DEJA DREW

BRIEFS AND BOXERS: A SELECTION OF SHORTS

DREW SNELL

Front Cover Art by Jimmy Pereira, jimmydraws4u@gmail.com

Tossin Tomaters, LLC

ALSO BY DREW SNELL:

BELLY-UP

To The Three Musketeers

ACKNOWLEDGMENTS

My heartfelt thanks to my wife Robin for her love, for her tenure, and mostly, for her patience.

My sincere thanks to Kathy Nicklaus Adkins the original Publisher and Editor of Lakeland Heartbeat Magazine who took a chance on a horse all those years ago.

I owe sincere thanks also to Mona Jackson, the magazine's succeeding Publisher, as well as Editor Dina Jackson, and to K.C. Jarrett, my late friend and fellow writer. It was a suggestion from the Jackson sisters and their support which led to the creation of the potentially provocative Tossin' Tomaters column which I wrote for many years.

My thanks and love also to the good people of Lakeland, Florida.

Like any good, albeit a "somewhat older boy", I must thank Miss Gray, my sixth-grade English teacher who taught me Iambic Pentameter. That words, like music, have a beat.

CONTENTS

INTRODUCTION

Back in my early twenties, interviewing a potential employee, I asked why he'd left his previous job, to which he replied, "Shots!".

I didn't understand, so he repeated "Shots! Unloading a truck with shots!"

Still unable to grasp his explanation, I turned to his wife. "Shots!" she yelled, gesturing downward toward her lower body.

"I got fy-id for wearin' shots," he shouted, frustrated with my speed of interpretation.

From his accent, apparently, he and his dear wife were from somewhere up New England way, whereas I was not.

This book is a collection of another type of shots – or "shorts" as we refer to them, a bit closer to the equator. Written shorts. Many of which were previously published during a near-decade-long stint I had writing for Heartbeat Magazine in Lakeland, Florida. Hence the book's title, Deja Drew.

The "Briefs and Boxers: A Selection of Shorts" subtitle refers to the fact that while a lot of the anecdotes are brief and are endeavored to be tinged with humor, others are not. Some may even have an edge and might even throw a pugilistic jab or two at the subject or subject matter.

The book is a gathering of material from printed and published pages found in old cardboard boxes, two computers and new material which has been written since the magazine ceased publication.

The last piece in this book was written for what was to be the final issue of the magazine but which was never published as the magazine unexpectedly ceased publication one month earlier than the target date. It was included here as it seems a fitting close to this book.

Drew Snell

SWFL
   2025

PART 1
REAL-LIFE ADVENTURES

ONE

MY SUMMER VACATION

A TRUE STORY OF AVIATIONAL COURAGE
AND INVOLUNTARY FOOD DISPLACEMENT

"Bandits at twelve o'clock!" shouted the garbled voice through the pre—stereo headphones. "Bandits at twelve o 'clock!"

Suddenly, I could hear the ominous drone of a well—tuned, diving German Messerschmidt fighter aircraft as it fired its machine guns, "Rat—tat—tat—tat—tat!"

"Rat—tat—tat—tat—tat—tat!" came our tail gunner's fiery, leaded reply.

Well, okay. Maybe we didn't even have a tail gunner. Maybe this wasn't even the 1940's. Maybe I wasn't even born in the 1940's. Maybe it was decades past the 1940's. Maybe I was having "12 0 ' Clock High" TV series flashbacks. But I WAS in a plane.

We were skimming along the surface of the Atlantic Ocean, just off the coast of South Florida, courtesy of the two flotation pods of the tiny, five passenger seaplane we had chartered for an island hop. The little, single engine plane was straining to pull up, off the water and become airborne as the pilot pulled back on his stick. We were attempting to leave the immediate vicinity of Key West's highest point – the city dump.

Eeeeeeeeyaaaawwwww ... strained the little plane.

"Everybody lean forward!" shouted the pilot over the straining clamor of the engine, as he heeded his own command. The five of us passengers exchanged uneasy glances

and followed his lead, as I began to regret my breakfast selection an hour earlier of a "short stack" of leaded cement patties, cleverly marketed as "pancakes". Perhaps if I'd had

something lighter like say, a large pink Pepto Bismol shake with a Dramamine chaser.

Was leaning forward standard aviational procedure? I didn't recall any of the other pilots ever telling their passengers to lean forward in any episodes of "12 0 'Clock High". In fact, I didn't recall them even having any passengers. Maybe that's why they never told

anyone to lean forward.

If this winged, motorized claustrophobic can gave up and suddenly cartwheeled across the top of the water, it would make a considerable "divot" in our family clan.

Typically, Cousin Randy was in the co—pilot seat. I was seated directly behind him, trying to suck in fresh air from the one-inch gap allowed by my vented window. My cousin Mick, Randy's brother, was seated behind me, clutching his camera, wondering if he had taken his last photo – ever. Cousin Cindy, their sister was seated directly across the eight-inch aisle from me, clutching onto her seat. Randy's wife Mary was quietly seated directly behind Cindy.

"Eeeeeeyyaaaaawwww! " strained the little plane. The plane finally nosed off the water and then slapped back down. This happened several times, until finally, we were airborne, climbing, then banking away from the imposing shadow and the pungent aroma of "Mount Trashmore", and the lovely, tropical island of Key West.

A beautiful, tropical, summer morning sun streamed through the windshield of the finally airborne, winged sardine can. Suddenly, I noticed what appeared to be tropical motor oil splashing up onto the plane's windshield from somewhere beneath the plane's hood. Was this also standard aviational procedure? Whenever things like this happened on "12 0 ' Clock High" it was just before one of the engines caught fire and they went into a downward tailspin. We only had one engine. I began to peer around for a fire extinguisher.

The pilot and Randy of course had an up close and personal view of the oil sliming up the windshield. The pilot began talking feverishly into the microphone on his headset. He had the advantage over us. He could make his own funeral arrangements ahead of time. I began peering downward at the distant water below, trying to recall my adolescent high dive techniques. Suddenly, the plane lurched left.

"What is it? What's wrong?" Mary shouted over the drone of the engine. (Note: prop planes drone; jets roar). Mary now saw the oil slick on the windshield and the pilot turned on the windshield wipers as they madly began to slap temporary visual clearings through the black effervescent pool of the escaping Middle East-based slimy substance.

"We're going down!" shouted Randy, with a touch of twisted melodrama, reminiscent of old, annoying, "Airport" movie sequels.

"We 've got a bit of a problem," countered the pilot,

"We're going back to base."

The pilot banked the plane sharply to the right, back toward the lovely, tropical isle of Key West. As we rolled right, so did Cindy's eyes, her facial complexion taking on the lovely, tropical hue of "Yoda green".

Minutes later, we landed safely upon the ocean at Garrison Bight, just outside of Key West. For Cindy, it was too late.

I don't mean that she had expired. I mean that HER BREAKFAST had "expired"

right into the accommodating beach towel on her lap.

"We either blew a gasket, or those crazy kids who changed the oil last night forgot to put the oil cap back on," the pilot speculated, although at that point, no one was particularly interested. He beached the craft and a bug—eyed Cindy clawed her way over the top of everyone to get out of the plane.

The pilot left to search out his "crazy" adolescent ground crew, while the rest of us calmly and quietly exited the plane, knelt upon the earth, and kissed it "Hello", just as we had almost kissed a portion of our anatomy "Goodbye" a few minutes before.

TWO

BIKE GEEK AT BIKE WEEK

I used to be a biker. I must say that there is nothing quite like it. The freedom. The fresh air. The thrill of the open road. The unharnessed wind rushing at your face. The pavement hurling past, beneath your feet as you pedal down the street.

That was back when tough guys rode Schwinn's, puffed on no-filter candy cigarettes, and the only piece of leather they owned was their Little League baseball glove.

When I was a kid, I had always wanted a motorbike. Unfortunately, this desire was not ever contingent with family corporate policy.

Being a true rebel and a renegade, when I achieved the legal age of 21, I still yearned for my own motorized two-wheel transportation. When a co-worker conveniently happened to have a used Yamaha 50cc dirt bike for sale, I quickly came up with the cash.

As motorcycle enthusiasts will note, if converted to a kitchen appliance application, the power of a 50cc engine would peak at puree. But it was a motorbike, and it was mine.

As I was still living at home with the folks, I conveniently managed to smuggle my motorized Japanese acquisition into the garage at a time when they weren't home.

"What's that out in the garage?" my father asked me, shortly after their arrival home.

"Why, uh whatever do you mean?" I responded nervously.

"Either it goes, or you do."

Fortunately, it took an entire month to find a buyer. This allowed my brother and myself the opportunity to ride the bike through many orange groves. It also allowed us the opportunity to get thrown out of most of them.

It was the bike's high-pitched, incessant whining that alerted grove owners of our unlawful trespass.

If Japanese motorcycles are "whiners", American built

Harley-Davidsons are "thunderous bass baritones with phossilized phlem".

Being a veteran Schwinn biker, and a 30-day veteran Yamaha biker, I felt a natural calling to visit the (motorized - as in BIG) bike-swarming streets of Daytona Beach during Bike Week.

As any veteran biker like me knows, one does not simply "go" to Bike Week in Daytona. One must "arrive with an attitude" at Bike Week in Daytona. It is an attitude which only we veteran bikers can understand - a hardened attitude acquired from hard living. From living our lives on the edge.

Personal appearance is very important to biker persons. We must wear lots of black, rebellious clothing. Each of us must also wear more hot, sweaty, leather than a stampeding herd of Texas Longhorns in a John Wayne movie.

Our overall appearances are testimonies to the tough (i.e. leathery) lives we lead. For instance, the morning of my visit to Bike Week, I stood up against the

"sheared-establishment" by calling up and rebelliously cancelling my scheduled hair appointment, in order that my hair would continue to have that wild, rebellious look, nearly touching the tops of my ears.

That morning, I purposely shaved my face with an electric razor, so I'd obtain a roughly shaven, somewhat micro-stubbled look.

I scuffed up my oldest pair of black cowboy boots, and wrinkled my only black shirt, and pulled them all on. I leered rudely into the full-length mirror, trying to project a tough biker motif. But there was something missing.

As I was opposed to any permanent, indelible ink markings upon my person, I quickly visited a local temporary tattoo parlor and selected a tattoo. Wanting to obtain some of the realism (i.e. pain) of acquiring a real tattoo, after some discussion, and some additional cash, I managed to persuade the tattoo artist (applicator) to iron the temporary tattoo onto my right forearm. I must say that with the iron-on application my tattoo achieved some extra longevity, and I achieved a rather high degree of pain.

To find Daytona, all I had to do was steer toward the northeast and follow the thunder — the thunder of a few hundred thousand Harley's as they roared through the streets.

Once I had shamefully hidden my car, and began mingling with the black-shirted, black-leathered biker crowd strolling along Main Street, I re-acquired my tough 50cc biker attitude. Occasionally, I jaywalked. I didn't always say "please" and "thank you" whenever applicable. When I yawned, I didn't always cover my mouth.

The bikes were parked side-by-side along both sides of Main Street. They were beautiful and alluring. So were a lot of the women (a.k.a. "biker chicks"). Several biker chick women took advantage of the warm spring day by wearing fashionable, black leather T-backs with complimentary black lace hose, decorated with black lace flowers, the Harley-Davidson logo, or with a tasteful collection of black-laced miniature skulls.

I walked by an amiably appearing establishment named "The Swine Pit", as I

began my quest to find Main Street's infamous "Boot Hill Saloon".

After walking toward the ocean until my newly purchased hat (black and leather, of course) nearly floated, I turned around, traversing what seemed to be a mile or two, back in the direction from which I had come, and found Boot Hill Saloon as advertised: appropriately, across the street from the cemetery.

Even though it has been a while since I stood amongst the Boot Hill Saloon patrons sipping an adult beverage, gazing upward at the colorful collection of ladies undergarments dangling from the rafters, as the band appropriately played the 1960's hit "House of The Rising Sun", I must say that a portion of the trip is still with me.

I'm pleased to say that I seem to have really gotten my money's worth with that temporary tattoo. Bugs is still holding up well. But the carrot is in trouble.

THREE
A TAIL OF TWO RODENTS

"It was the best of times. It was the worst of times," mused Marlon Parkins, famous and aged backyard outdoorsman from the security and sanctity of his heavily screened back porch. We were seated at his patio table, sipping on a couple of cold adult beverages, as Parkins gazed wistfully outward, into the depths of his zero-lot line backyard, as he began to recall a true story which had occurred not so long ago.

Although I have been one of the retired, great man's personal friends for many years, I am still awed by his presence. Also, by the volume of backyard adventures which he relates.

Upon this particular occasion, Parkins began relating a story which he considered as having a best case, worst-case scenario. The "best" portion of the incident was coming to the aid of a lady in distress. The "worst" possibility being the potential elimination of one or maybe two members of his beloved wild kingdom.

The story involved a young, divorced woman named Ann who was living in a small, singlewide mobile home in the company of her six-year-old son. The setting was a rural one.

One evening, while lying in bed, Ann began hearing noises coming from the kitchen at the opposite end of the trailer. The sounds could best be described as the crumpling of snack bags, and the crunching of potato chips. The terrified woman locked her bedroom door, barricaded it with a chair, and pulled the bedcovers over her head and that of her young son who lay next to her, sound asleep.

The next morning, after having spent a sleepless night, Ann cautiously investigated the vacant, now silent kitchen. She found the pantry door open and a half-eaten bag of barbequed potato chips on the floor. After a thorough investigation of the kitchen, Ann summoned Jim Bob, her somewhat psychotic, over-zealous boyfriend, to the scene. His examination of the scene also proved to be fruitless, and his talk of potential gunplay did little to quell her fears.

Gradually, life returned to normal for Ann, although she would not enter the kitchen in the morning without first lobbing a few shoes into the room from the other side of the trailer in an attempt to frighten away her unseen, uninvited, nightly visitor.

A few evenings, and a few dozen shoes later, Ann and her son were once again lying in bed when she again heard the apparent crackling sounds of a snack bag coming from the pitch-black proximity of the kitchen. She sat bolt upright in bed, her heart racing, pumping both fear and adrenaline throughout her trembling body.

Ann summoned her courage and began quietly creeping down the blackened hallway toward the kitchen bravely armed with only a single, unforgiving shoe. The crackling sounds became louder as she approached the darkened kitchen. Her hand trembled nearly uncontrollably as she struggled to find, and then rotate the kitchen light dimmer switch, as she peered her head around the corner, into the kitchen.

Before Ann could turn the dimmer switch to its brightest position, she could make out a dark, furry, four-legged, furry-tailed creature in the dim light. Suddenly, it silently bolted across the floor, seemingly on its two hind legs, and disappeared, dashing behind an open cabinet door, and into the cabinet beneath the sink.

Ann screamed and raced back to the bedroom where she bolted and barricaded the door. After a panicked call to Jim Bob, he arrived promptly. After making certain that the uninvited evening visitor had truly departed, they discovered that the ambitious creature had dragged an entire loaf of bread from the pantry to a potential dining area behind the stove.

Yet, after much investigation, they could not figure out just how the furry visitor had entered and exited the skirted abode.

The next evening, Jim Bob positioned himself on the living room couch. A grateful Ann and son turned off the kitchen and living room lights and barricaded themselves in the bedroom for the night. That evening, and for many evenings to follow, nothing happened.

Then one night, when Jim Bob was weaponless and asleep, sprawled out on the living room couch, he awakened to the sound of a cabinet door slamming shut, followed by the sounds of a snack bag rustling. Jim Bob snatched up Ann's son's nearby popgun, threw on the kitchen light and shuddered at the scene before him.

Not six feet away, amongst an open bag of Lays Potato Chips, peering upward into Jim Bob's fearful, beer-bleary eyes was a startled, very much annoyed, skunk.

Jim Bob yelled, tossed the popgun aside, and sprinted down the hallway, arms a-flailing, toward the bedroom end of the trailer, nearly knocking over a curious Ann as she emerged from her bedroom.

Although the skunk never appeared in the trailer again after Jim Bob successfully sealed the creature's apparent entry route along some plumbing pipes which came up from under the trailer and into the kitchen cabinet.

After a pause, Marlon Parkins drew in a breath and began to relate a second curious rodent perpetrated incident which occurred to Ann a few weeks later.

She had been having car trouble with her ancient, General Motors manufactured Buick and took it to her mechanic for him to repair. After examining the car, the mechanic directed Ann's attention to a severed engine hose, carefully pointing out what distinctly appeared to be the gnaw marks of a rodent.

Parkins was quick to dismiss Ann's Buick engine hose incident as being the act of a vindictive, potato chips, and bread eating skunk, as he did not believe wild animals to be capable of such destructive retaliation. Yet, he was excited by the potential marketing campaign which could be built upon the Buick hose-chewing rodent.

"Imagine!" he exclaimed excitedly. "Just imagine how valuable such a rodent would be to the folks at General Motors Corporation!"

"How's that?"

"Imagine! A rodent which prefers Genuine GM Parts!"

FOUR

THE BIRD IS THE WORD

My fiancé's name (now wife) is Robin. When it comes to objects of home décor, her selections tend to be ornithological in nature. Bird pictures, bird statues, bird toys, bird teapots, bird cups, bird glasses, bird magnets, and bird drapes. Like the lyrics of that old 1960's surfing song, "The bird is the word" at Robin's house. So much so that when she was shopping for a house for herself several years ago and found one featuring a birdhouse wallpaper border in the master bedroom, she interpreted it as a sign and promptly bought the house - for a song. Give or take a few thousand dollars.

From that moment, the master bedroom's birdhouse wallpaper border figuratively rose in stature to a state nearing residential reverence. It became the proud pinnacle of all home tours which Robin conducted for certain houseguests, during which she verbally and enthusiastically recounted the cultural significance of the birdhouse border in influencing her purchase of the house. The famed birdhouse border was often the first object which she would see when her eyes fluttered open in the morning and was often the last thing she would see at the end of the day, just before turning out the light and closing her eyes to sleep.

A year or two after her home purchase, to my great horror, while attempting to protect her beloved birdhouse border as I performed a complimentary paint job of her master bedroom for which I was neither professionally licensed, nor insured, nor paid, I unwittingly ripped her revered, wallpaper border to shreds.

Manila-colored painter's tape is apparently produced in two adhesive persuasions: one which gently releases its grip upon its subject when tugged; and two, it's polarized, yet identically appearing, diabolical twin which seizes its victim with a Godzilla-like death grip, potentially capable of ripping out the heartily rooted eyebrow crop of a uni-browed, day spa-bound wildebeest with a single, excruciating yank. I ignorantly and unsuspectingly purchased the lethal manila coiled "painters' tape" at a local building materials store. Upon my return, I unwittingly encircled the upper perimeter of her bedroom birdhouse border with the Godzilla grip tape, draping large, numerous sheets of newspaper pages from the lower edge of the tape, in an effort to carefully shield her beloved wallpaper border from soon to be spattering paint.

Aside from my breaking the hand off an angel statue, dripping paint onto the carpet, and shattering the globe of a neighboring ceiling light fixture, the actual paint job itself was pretty much uneventful. Of course, ripping my fiancé's birdhouse wallpaper border to shreds did cast somewhat of a pall over my completed job. Although I had never wallpapered in my life, upon my unintentional, complimentary demolition of her beloved border, I felt that it would be in my best interest to take up the trade. Promptly.

After lengthy experimentation I somehow managed to mix the glue and to get the new border which Robin had selected to adhere over the ragged remnants of the revered original, thoroughly concealing my crime. Yet, I must admit that throughout the tedious process, the glue exhibited a continuous habit which I plan on implementing the next time someone attempts to get me to paint or to wallpaper their house. That would be, run.

FIVE

TOSSING INK

While it will come as an incomprehensible shock to anyone who has been subjected to my written ramblings over the years, I was once employed in the newspaper business. I tossed 'em. As a circulation department district manager back in the day, whenever one of the ten newspaper carriers in my district was sick or quit, I was the guy who made certain that all of the two or three hundred subscribers on the route received their morning papers on time and without interruption, until the carrier had either recovered, or had been replaced.

Back then, morning newspaper carriers enjoyed a unique, nocturnal, outdoor working environment and a culture all their own, often sleeping when we're awake and waking when we're asleep, sometimes meeting and socializing amongst themselves during midnight breakfasts at all night restaurants, before picking up their papers for the morning's delivery. For the most part, newspaper carriers were diligent, unheralded, hardworking folks. As in all occupations, there are exceptions. My exception's name was a guy named Gus.

Gus was in his early forties, a flagrantly chunky fellow, six feet tall, his greasy, balding, dandruff-strewn black hair combed straight back from his ample forehead. He was an unmarried chain smoker whose natural, rather pungent, unwashed aroma flagrantly exhibited an apparent aversion to entertaining an aromatically acceptable level of personal hygiene, a practice which not only consistently and successfully challenged the maximum irritational capacity of my tear ducts, but also my appetite for lunch.

One morning, via the rather substantial volume of telephone calls from perturbed subscribers on Gus's route, we quickly determined that Gus had apparently not delivered his route, so I drove to his telephoneless apartment to investigate. Outside his apartment at nine a.m., I found his unattended car loaded with a couple hundred newspapers, bagged and ready for delivery on the backseat.

I knocked on the apartment door. No answer, but suddenly the volume of the TV I could hear from within lowered and the murmuring conversation I could also hear from within, ceased.

"Come on Gus, I know you're in there," I shouted. "Why didn't you run your route? We've got lots of angry customers calling the office wanting to know what happened! We gotta get those papers delivered !" I pounded on the door again and finally heard the door unlock from within.

Slowly, cautiously, the apartment door swung open, while a powerful, knee-buckling chemical stench burst outward, rushing up into my unprepared nostrils. As I gasped for air, and collected my balance, I visually took in the scene. Gus's younger, long-haired buddy had opened the door. His eyes were bloodshot and glazed, his face ashen, frozen in a goofy grin.

Gus was seated on a stuffed chair toward the center of the room, facing me, his seemingly uncooperative hands clumsily managing to shove a small, clear, plastic baggie containing a flattened small tube into concealment beneath the accommodating skirt of his chair. He then gazed upon me, with his stoned, bloodshot eyes, pulling his mouth into a moronic, sheepish grin, the upper lip of which was bordered with a generous bead of what I could only surmise to be Testor's finest model airplane glue.

Somehow, Gus went on to deliver his newspapers that day. Shortly after the recreational glue incident, I chose to leave the newspaper circulation profession. I just couldn't stick with it.

SIX

PLEASE DON'T EAT THE PANSIES

As I did not get married until late in life, I am a bit hesitant to reveal that the pansy is my favorite flower. Did I also happen to mention that I do not attend ballets or operas, and that I love John Wayne and Bruce Willis movies?

As it does in the cases of many men, it has taken me much of my life to finally derive some kind of pleasure from our botanical friends. This is because in our society, the male's historical interactive role with vegetation involves a lawn mower, a weed wacker, and an edger.

Until recently, the only vegetative interaction which I actually enjoyed consisted of a series of unlimited visits to the salad bar at the Golden Corral Steakhouse. But as I've gotten older, for the most part, I have found my backyard encounters amid the flora and fauna to be relaxing. Again, for the most part ...

There have been exceptions. Like the time I was surveying my backyard to determine if there was any lawn left amongst the healthy multitude of weeds. Suddenly an object on the ground near my foot caught my eye. At first glance, the object appeared to be serpentine, coiled, and taste-testing the air in my immediate vicinity with a forked, flickering tongue. I swallowed hard and forced myself to look downward again and stared with wide-eyed disbelief at the triangularly-headed snake of multi-cultural coloring, and of moderate length. At just about that moment, in a sudden, unrehearsed but incredibly sincere attempt to break the Olympic record for the standing high jump, I sprang straight up in the air for several hundred feet. I was more than terribly disappointed when I felt myself beginning to descend.

My feet were already moving before I hit the ground. When they did hit, the momentum from my churning Chucks propelled me into the sanctity of an upright, unyielding wooden fence, while the snake swiftly slithered away, disappearing into some bushes.

Upon entering my backyard one day a few weeks later, something didn't feel right.

Somehow it felt like I was in a slightly skewed promo for a "Jaws" movie sequel: "Just when you felt it was safe to go back into the backyard ...".

This time I was in a flower bed, yanking up some weeds when I thought I saw something very long, very black, and very snaky, stealthily slithering toward me through the grass. I looked up just in time to see a black snake the length of a city bus bearing down on me.

At the last minute, he turned and dashed into the bushes.

When my heart began beating again, I decided that after all, the bathroom probably

should be cleaned RIGHT AWAY.

BUT NO! I would be a man and stand my ground! This was MY backyard. Actually, I would run to the opposite side of the yard, very quickly plant a bush, then dash into the house and watch a John Wayne movie ... or something.

No sooner had I gotten to the other side of the yard when the huge black creature suddenly reappeared, lunging at me from the cover of a birdbath.

As I snatched up the shovel as a weapon, I flashed back to an old episode of Mutual of Omaha's Wild Kingdom where old Marlin Perkins was sitting safely in a studio in Omaha,

Nebraska while Jim, his younger, more active assistant, was standing in a pond somewhere being thoroughly thrashed about by a massive Anaconda snake.

As the ravenous, attacking anaconda wannabe in my backyard

lunged at me with mouth agape, I plunged the cold, unforgiving steel of the shovel head deep into his serpentine hide. Again and again, I diced him.

When I was done, I had cleaved that backyard anaconda into a multitude of proportions so brief, they would have made those folks in Vienna who make those short sausages mighty proud.

SEVEN
THE LOST WEEKEND

As a rule, the woman of the house has been overly generous in assigning everyday duties for the long-suffering, officially designated man of the house. This can result in the man carrying a heavy burden of responsibility. Aside from carrying out the trash, which can be a fairly heavy burden in itself, depending upon the cumulative weight of the discards.

An intelligent man of the house learns that despite his schooling and his personal aspirations, it is often in his best interest to rapidly become a competent actor, potentially capable of exuding performances worthy of an off-Broadway Oscar nomination. Particularly in the category of feigned enthusiasm over such femininely-enthralling topics as linen thread counts, drapery colors, in-law visits, and of course, one of my all-time favorites, family visits to Orlando theme parks. Against my better judgement and wishes, I recently found myself committed to the latter.

As billed, the event was to be an intimate weekend between my fiancé · the current reigning woman of the house, myself, an entourage of eight of our immediate kin, and a gaggle of several thousand multi-aged, fanny-packing, heartily-perspiring, sun scorched, citizens of the world.

Shortly after awakening from our first night's sleep at our Orlando motel, while rooting around for her morning things, my fiancé glumly announced that she had apparently lost her wallet. A thorough examination of the room, including a particularly unpleasant search segment upon our hands and middle-aged knees, substantiated her dismal declaration. She stated that she did not remember having her wallet when we had been at the theme park the previous day, and helpfully expanded the field of search by suggesting that she might have left her wallet at home, or perhaps some place else.

After eliminating a few of the more immediate "someplace else" locations, we drove the hour-plus home, thankfully found her wallet and then immediately drove the hour-plus back to our loyal, dutifully awaiting family entourage at the Orlando motel. Once reunited, we all went to the theme park where it promptly began to rain. A driving rain and the subsequently violent lightning storm not only forced us to seek cover, but also caused an extended electrical power loss, resulting in the closure of the park.

The next morning brought better weather, but not better luck. Shortly after showering, my fiancé announced that one of the hoop earrings I had bought her had fallen into the drain. While I peered cautiously downward into the dark, ominously yawning two-inch wide bacterial cauldron, contemplating the cost of a new pair of earrings, I considered the probable condition of the jeweled hoop: immersed in an antibiotically-impervious microbe swarming goo, the living cream-colored crud of a thousand complimentary oily motel mini soaps, mortaring together a multitude of assorted permanently-permed, germ-laden stalks of disembodied hair.

Minutes after assessing the situation, I dutifully strode through the motel lobby where my brother, cousin and their immediate families were completing their breakfasts like all the other normal, non-crisis impeded, motel guests. When I returned bearing a flashlight through the bright, sunlit lobby, they were intrigued. They recognized an opportunity for gratis, potential entertainment and enthusiastically followed me all the way back to the room. My anticipating, bemused audience of semi-immediate family quickly assembled themselves in and around the motel bathroom to view my MacGyver-esque efforts, as I awkwardly and fully clothed, climbed aboard the still wet, artic white bathtub.

Then, by applying a pair of eyebrow plucking forceps, the flashlight beam, some earnest grunts and a gifted series of physical contortions, I deftly, and somewhat wearily, managed to extract a single, hairy, cream-colored, soap-encrusted, hoop earring to the sound of cheers.

EIGHT
RODENTS ON THE RAMPAGE

If you listen carefully, you may hear a "swishing sound". This swishing sound is not American jobs going to Mexico.

Unfortunately, that swishing sound you're hearing is probably only a rat the size of a chihuahua doing the breaststroke in your bathroom toilet.

Admittedly, there may be cause for alarm if an aquatically inclined rodent exhibits an ability for holding its breath longer than Olympic Swim Team Champion Michael Phelps, by swimming through several hundred feet of sewer pipe in a successful, covert attempt to enter your house.

Unfortunately for Rat Olympians, there is one less aquatic rodent representing the USA these days. This is because many years ago, after one such dampened rodent athlete emerged from the ceramic vestibule of our family toilet, my father beat the stuffing out of him with a commandeered emergency house broom.

By nature, and by profession, another aquatically gifted rodent is the beaver. Beavers have bucked-teeth, swim, occasionally wear baseball caps, and constantly say "Gee Wally", while starring in 1960's TV shows.

When I was a boy, my dad would occasionally take me to a small, isolated pond in the woods where he kept a little wooden rowboat. We would row out into the middle of that pond and we'd often watch a family of wild, bareheaded beavers swimming, playing, and working on their dam for hours.

Looking back, I'm sure that the fond childhood memories I have of Dad and I being in that little rowboat seeded the marine interest I have today.

Apparently, I was not the only one who harbored an enthusiastic interest for boats and boating. That family of beavers also took a liking to my dad's boat.

In fact, they liked it so much that one day they had it for lunch.

The portions of the cannibalized craft which they did not digest, the buck-toothed, flat-tailed rodents incorporated into the superstructure of their dam.

Although I was but a youngster, I can still recall Dad's immediate reaction to the beavers eating his boat. He pretty well wore out the words "Beavers" and "Dam" though not necessarily in that particular order.

Recently, there has been another alarming incident involving rodents. This time, involving squirrels. Squirrels can be defined as spastic, chattering, nut—gathering, bushy—tailed, tree—dwelling rodents, or possibly, as Orville Overbite from the mailroom.

One particular squirrel of the bush-tailed variety which we will call "Tinkle" has been tormenting a friend of mine whom we will call "Ted". Much to Ted's dismay Tinkle has been leaving multitudes of personalized "gifts" all over Ted's yard, the interior of his garage, and all over his previously white, patio furniture.

Ted describes the "residue" which Tinkle leaves behind as a "disgustingly brown, syrupy substance".

For months, Ted annoyedly observed Tinkle going into his open garage and tearing multiple holes in stored bags of Dog Chow, and then blatantly dining on the spilled contents.

After sweeping and mopping up one too many of Tinkle's messes in the garage, Ted bought a small, metal garbage can in which to store all his dog's food. While his dog now happily has more food to eat, Ted reports that Tinkle is well, really peed off.

He reports (Ted, that is) that Tinkle has since left a flurry of multiple "gifts" all over the impenetrable metal trash can, in order to exhibit his extreme displeasure with Ted's new dog food storage technique.

In placing the food in a metal trash can, Ted has unintentionally taught Tinkle to do what mother nature apparently could not: how to use the can.

NINE
TORTUGA FLAT

TV commercials had been bugging me for years to do it. I finally did it. I went on a real, aquatic cruise.

Until then, my cruising experience had been limited to cruising for "chicks" a.k.a. "babes", a.k.a. "foxes", a.k.a. "women who wouldn't give me the time of day" along Fort Lauderdale Beach.

Unfortunately, women were hard to find aboard the particular cruise that I went on. In fact, there weren't any aboard at all.

At 5 P.M., the captain began to slowly back our sturdy, 20-year-old, red and white, 115-foot fishing vessel away from the rustic dock at Key West's Stock Island. Four beautiful ladies, most of them wives of some of our luckier shipmates, generously waved "goodbye", "good luck", and possibly "good riddance" to us for the next three days.

It was an emotional sight: the boat pulling away from the dock, amid the flutter of handheld handkerchiefs. We waved them at the smiling, hand-waving women, and used them to dry our tears in between waves.

After all, we were waving "goodbye" to land, women, cable TV, and personal hygiene for the next three days.

Of course, we still had beer. Forty-two cases of that most reverent, iced, hopped, and barleyed, guy-sustaining beverage. There were also several cases of assorted soft drinks, and 25 gallons of bottled water.

For the most part, we were 35 fishing guys strong. By the end of our three day, "forbidden to expend freshwater by showering" cruise, we 35 fishing guys were "strong" in another sense, as well.

As our hearty, beer-laden vessel raced away from Key West, toward the fishing grounds of the Dry Tortugas, about 70 miles away, we began to survey our floating, aquatic living conditions.

Although our accommodations were not plush, they were fishermanly adequate. Aboard the boat, our personal space was limited to human toaster slots. In fact, for the next three days, I felt like an unwashed Kellog's Pop Tart.

As we entered the long, narrow, main cabin from the back end (stern) of the boat, there were a series of slotted berths on either side of the long center aisle.

Each berth was about seven feet long, two feet high, and about four feet deep. Just enough for sleeping amongst your provisions-crammed gym bag, atop the three-inch-thick foam rubber mattress, covered with a single cover sheet, and accessorized with a miniature pillow. Blankets were something you brought from home.

We were stacked three high, and about eight long. The top rows of berths were accessed by ladders. The bottom row, by crawling on the floor.

Without too much trouble, I managed to select a lower berth which was not only accessed by crawling on the floor, but which also happened to be located directly over the engine room. An engine room in which the huge *twin* diesels were *never* turned off.

Also, by lucky coincidence, my berth also happened to be the nearest located to the heavy steel, bulkhead door which served as the main entrance and main exit to the bathrooms for the many door—clanging, beer-renting, inebriated, all night fishing men in our expedition.

Of course, to be nautically correct, bathrooms on boats are called "heads". Our vessel was equipped with two heads.

The "Economy Class Head" had a flushable toilet, a 12X12 inch soap-less sink, and if you were lucky, a portion of a roll of paper towels.

The "First Class Head" contained the same comforts as that in the Economy Class, but also had a mirror, a single bar of bone-dry, behaired Irish Spring Soap seemingly permanently stuck to the top of the sink. A small, single shower was adjacent to the sink, an overturned heavy duty toilet plunger upon its floor at the ready, pitching and rolling upon the whim of the sea.

Fortunately, the whims and the winds were gracious. There was very little wind, and very little waves. The sea was pretty much flat.

The only true breaks in the water were made by the splash of fishing weights.

One of my nearby fishing companions was quite adept at this. He was a young, dark-haired young man whom the captain should have dubbed "Clicker".

His over-ballasted fishing lines captured our trip's record number of Moray Eels. No matter his prey or his posture, Clicker always left his reel on "heavy drag" which made even his shortest, least resisted, bait-checking reel-ins sound like he was battling Moby Dick.

"Click! Click! Click! Click! "

After three days of subtle, and not-so-subtle "suggestions" by the captain to Clicker, to simply turn-off his reel's drag, the captain, a colorful (in language and in demeanor), pony-tailed sort, began to get annoyed.

Clicker just didn't get it.

Oddly enough, neither my fishing companion nor I could locate Clicker aboard the boat on the way in. I'm betting he's spending a whole lot more time with those Moray's than he wanted too.

TEN
REAL WILD KINGDOM

My most recent exhilarating wildlife encounter occurred while I was pushing the lawnmower around the backyard, pondering as to whether or not the inventor of the pith helmet harbored a lisp when I was suddenly and deliberately stung upon my "hindquarters" (a Real Wild Kingdom-esque term) by a venomous, and ill-mannered insect.

Two weeks later, I had completely recovered, and was working in my backyard, when I was suddenly stung upon my left wrist. I ran inside the house and attended the injury with legal, though not necessarily learned, substances which included ice, a small tub of Parkay Margarine, a yard of mint-flavored dental floss, and a seven-ounce bottle of Mennen Skin Bracer.

Half an hour later, I stubbornly returned to the scene of my attack, determined to finish the job I had started. A minute later, I was stung between the thumb and forefinger of my right hand.

As I rapidly retreated for the safety of my house, I could not help but make several earnest, yet ill-willed gesticulations in the direction of my attackers with my matched set of painfully swelling hands.

Several days later, I had recovered both my original, respective hand sizes, and enough of my courage to return to the safety, security, and air conditioning, of my enclosed back porch. There, over a cool, refreshing beverage, I observed what appeared to be some sort of an insectic swarming at the base of a short brick wall which supported a fern bed.

I perilously pressed my nose upon the glass of a nearby window. What were those? Flies…?

With my vast knowledge and experience of the Real Wild Kingdom, it only took me milli-seconds of observing several hundred members of the wasp-like creatures darting into the air at a 45-degree angle from a hole in the ground to realize that the insects were probably not of the common house fly variety.

After observing the first thousand or so angry, stinger-armed, insectic kamikazes swarming out of the hole, I concluded that any initial challenge regarding their unauthorized use of my backyard airspace would have to involve something a bit more substantial than a twelve ounce can of Raid Yard Guard.

As bugs and painful stings were not my gig, I called in a trained professional. A young, personable man arrived in a bee suit and sprayed a chemical gas up the earthen entry way of the swarming, insectic abode.

While he was attacked by the angry, black and yellow ringed insectic vermin, he was unharmed as his suit absorbed their normally excruciating stings. He began to dig into the top of the fern bed with a shovel.

Minutes later, he unearthed a multi-storied, football-sized and football-shaped yellow jacket nest. He permanently quelled the nest's swarming, enraged guardians and inhabitants with a few pints of swiftly lethal insecticide.

After I'd performed a vindictive happy dance upon the top story of the former yellow jacket hotel, and began writing the efficient young man a check, my thoughts drifted back to the stinging initial incident which had caused all of this.

Like people, sometimes insects can be a real pain in the hindquarters.

ELEVEN
OUR LADY OF SEMINOLE FINANCE (1996)

Most of the truly amazing things I have seen in my life, I have been able to attribute to Walt Disney. Until now.

I don't put much stock in fruits and vegetables which are claimed to be naturally shaped images of movie stars, or in cinnamon rolls that are alleged to look like Mother Theresa, or even in billboard advertisements for spaghetti in which some observers claim to be able to see the face of Jesus Christ.

Yet, in December 1996 curiosity caused me to drive my fiancé and myself to Clearwater, in an attempt to find the well-publicized, alleged image of The Virgin Mary which had mysteriously appeared on the side of an office building.

I'd already heard many opinions on the controversial image. Many of them from people who'd never even attempted to see it. Didn't need to. It was fake. It was real. They'd already made up their minds without leaving the comfort of their living room chairs.

Some of the more hearty of the armchair folks declared that they would not allow themselves to be affected by the appearance of any religious image which did not prove to be that of Jesus Christ, or of God, Himself. Tough room.

The most common scientific reason I'd heard for the image's

appearance was that it was caused by water stains on the windows from the building's outdoor sprinkler system.

Still another, was that the glass in the windows was insulated and that the gas between the layers of glass had leaked out, causing the image to form.

Although it had been years since either my fiancé or I had been to Clearwater, we found the busy intersection where the image was located without incident. Given my naturally defective sense of direction, I did not entirely rule out divine intervention.

There were police officers helping people cross the street. Three ambulances and a TV news van were parked in a nearby parking lot, as were a line of porta-potti's.

The parking lot alongside The Seminole Finance Building was devoid of vehicles. Several hundred people stood in near silence, looking upward at a silent, still image posed upon nine large panes of glass, seemingly looking downward at them.

The gathering of people was of all ages, of all backgrounds, in visibly various states of health. There were people in wheelchairs, people with aluminum walkers, people leaning upon others for physical support. There were people in awe, people in deep thought, people in prayer, people with goosebumps.

Hundreds of flowers and candles, and dozens of photographs, and scraps of paper with personal, penciled prayers addressed to "The Virgin Mary" lined the lengthy, three-foot retaining wall before the image.

Toward the front of the crowd, a petite, older woman silently held aloft a large, framed painting of The Virgin Mary, slowly rotating it, for all the crowd and for all the world, to see. A silent, magnificently powerful testimony of her faith as to the origin, and the identity of the image on the glass.

A group of a dozen, seemingly devout, middle-aged Hispanic persons quietly chanted what must have been a Hispanic prayer over and over again. The only discernible, often-repeated word I could make out, being "Maria".

The atmosphere was somewhat eerie, somewhat surreal, peaceful, and wonderful. There were no financial gains to be made here. No dishonesty. No ulterior motives. Only a common cause. A sense of unity; of togetherness, amongst the crowd.

The image had appeared on that portion of the building which gave it the greatest visibility to the most people.

If the image is, in fact, The Virgin Mary, why would she appear on a finance building? A little girl quoted on a TV newscast tells us "God is trying to tell us that we care too much about money".

Scientific explanations? Sure. Even so, given the scientific factors, why did the outline happen to appear as one which is so easily interpreted to be that of The Virgin Mary?

We also have scientific explanations for rainbows, for Noah's Flood, and for the Star of Bethlehem. We will always have them. They will always be easy outs for disbelievers.

What it all comes down to is to what kept that woman holding up that painting of The Virgin Mary. To faith.

I gotta tell you, I've been looking for spaghetti billboards ever since.

PART 2
AMERICANA

TWELVE
AMERICANA PIE

Several years after high school, I happily and unexpectedly found myself once again behind the wheel of Dad's white 1966 Ford Mustang Coupe. He lent me the car while my car was in the repair shop.

Dad had owned the car since 1972. While the car had a 2-barrel carburetor, an automatic transmission, with a 289 V-8 engine, it always had a tendency to be light in the rear end, so we kept a couple of bags of sand in the trunk for ballast.

Flashing back to 1972, I could still remember being too excited to sleep the night dad had given me permission to drive the Mustang to high school the next day. Today, the only way I can stay up all night thinking about a car is figuring out how I'm going to make the next car payment or pay its repair bills. Or both.

Until that wonderful carefree day back in high school in 1972, my brief, yet somewhat illustrious driving tenure had been restricted to occasional trips in the family station wagon. Squares-ville!

By driving that white 1966 Sports Car into that high school parking lot back in 1972, for a few precious moments I became something I'd been trying to be my whole adolescent life. I became cool. Certain cars can do that to guys.

They still can. No matter our age. Even a somewhat hefty, "vintage" multi-year-old guy like me can still feel cool, sliding behind the wheel of a "vintage" 60-year-old car which was not only such a large, important part of his youth, but which also became an American Classic.

Over fifty years later, the car is still a part of our family. My brother and I inherited the car after our dad passed. A few years later, I bought out my brother's half and now proudly have the car parked in my garage.

Some days just looking at it out in the garage is pleasure enough. Some days I gotta hear the baritone vibrato of that throaty engine roaring down the street. Either way, it just can't be that this is the same 1966 white Mustang that I used to drive to high school as a skinny sixteen-year-old kid in 1972. But it is.

To date the car has been a part of our family for fifty-four years. It has been our treasured, personal slice of Americana.

Appropriately, a nearly identical white Ford Mustang (a 1965) was featured on the cover of a 1986 Beach Boys record album entitled "Made In U.S.A.", by the band. A band which is official billed as "America's Band". You can't get yourself a much bigger slice of Americana than that.

THIRTEEN

BEACH BOYS, PLUS ONE

I'm a little older than I'd care to admit and I'm a member of a fan club. For many years, I 've been a member of the B.B.F.C. - the official fan club of The Beach Boys.

In my heart, I've always considered myself to be an unofficial, "unchartered member" of The Beach Boys, while personally taking their songs to new, "unchartered octaval heights" while singing along with their records.

My more memorable personal performances of Beach Boys songs occurred in the 70's, while I was attending college. I was living in an off-campus house with two male roommates who were not always apprecia-tive of my personal renditions of Beach Boys songs.

In the evenings, I'd often pull on a pair of stereo headphones, slip one of my Beach Boys albums onto the turntable, and quickly find myself musically immersed in the lush, harmonic waves of sound created by The Beach Boys.

Moments later, I'd be passionately singing along with their harmonies, my headphones shutting out all of the perfectly pitched musical keys, tones, and crescendos which I was confident that I was hitting.

My roommates often acknowledged my gratis performances by

quietly entering the room, spinning around, dropping their drawers and bending over in an unsolicited "celestial salutation"; in effect, mooning me for my musical efforts. In essence, responding to my musical exhibition with an expressive exhibition of their own.

But a truly dedicated artist does not allow the anatomical gesticulations of a couple of "cheeky" cynics to interfere with his vast musical talents, nor with his inevitable musical destiny.

My favorite concert performance was several years back at the Youkey theater in Lakeland Florida, where the acoustics were great, and where mooning the performers, and would-be performers, is illegal.

From my front row seat, for an hour and a half, I uninhibitedly performed many of the classic songs of The Beach Boys, in the musical accompaniment of the actual Beach Boys themselves, during their concert there. Okay, maybe the Beach Boys didn't necessarily look like "Boys" anymore. But then, neither did I. Neither did a lot of the members of the crowd.

Like most baby boomers, I grew up with The Beach Boys. And often in a very public, very painful way, they grew up with us. Through their lives, their music, and their longevity, they have become a large part of Americana. Moreover, they have helped define it.

During their 60 plus years as a musical group, The Beach Boys have experienced a series of tragedies, setbacks, rifts, rows, and fragmentations. They have endured it all because they are much more than a band: they are a family.

The Beach Boys originally began in 1961 as three teenage brothers: Brian, Dennis, and Carl Wilson, their cousin, Mike Love, and their good friend, Al Jardine.

After creating, producing, and arranging dozens of incredible, sunny, soul-lifting, hit songs in a six-year period, big brother Brian left the group after his fragile mental well-being fell casualty to the demands of an unscrupulous record industry, personal pressures, and to a devastating, smorgasbord of drugs.

Shortly thereafter, their good friend and solidly established recording artist Bruce Johnston joined the group to fill in for Brian.

Tragically, Dennis Wilson died in 1983, brother Carl Wilson in 1998.

Through his music, Brian Wilson has brought happiness to millions of people. One can only hope that despite his physical and mental health challenges, the deaths of his two brothers and his wife's passing in 2024, that somewhere along the way that Brian was able to find his own personal happiness, or at least, his own peace.

Sixty plus years have proven nearly all of The Beach Boys recordings to be timeless. Songs which celebrate a happiness and an innocence which many of us boomers thought we'd long since left behind. Songs which take us back to a time when our lives were a whole lot simpler. To a time when the most important things in our lives were girls, boys, cars, and beaches.

Songs which are just as pertinent to the lives of young people today as they were to young people 60 years ago.

At that Lakeland concert the crowd consisted of people of all ages, of different generations, all smiling, laughing, singing, and dancing together. All to the soaring, upbeat music of America's Band: The Beach Boys.

The reason was simple, really. Through their music, Brian Wilson and The Beach Boys have managed to do what Mark Twain did when he wrote "Tom Sawyer" and "Huckleberry Finn".

They have captured youth.

FOURTEEN
WESTERNS HO!

Whenever life gets a little too complicated, I like to watch a Classic Western Movie. I learned that from my dad.

All his life dad loved watching Westerns. Westerns starring Gary Cooper, Randolph Scott, Jimmy Stewart, Henry Fonda, Clint Eastwood, and of course, John Wayne.

For fifty years I watched and enjoyed the Best of the West alongside of him, never thinking to ask why he loved watching Westerns; why he preferred them to all the other types of movies.

When it finally occurred to me to ask, he thought for a moment before he replied.

"Simplicity. Times were a lot simpler back then. You've got the good guy and you've got the bad guys. It's pretty easy to tell who's who and what's what. Not like some other kinds of movies."

As for myself, I attribute one of the greatest movie lines ever, to a Western. The movie is the original "True Grit" starring John Wayne as the gritty, ornery Marshall Rooster J. Cogburn.

The likes of Lucky Ned Pepper (a younger Robert Duval) and a few of his evil cohorts are mounted atop their stationary horses, shoulder to shoulder, facing down Cogburn across an open field. Cogburn is alone on the opposite side of the field, mounted atop Bo his ever-faithful horse as he challenges them.

Their shouted, somewhat respectful conversation takes an ugly turn when Cogburn states that it is his intention to see Ned and his gang hanged in nearby Fort Smith.

Ned shouts back something about that being "Bold talk from a one-eyed fat man."

At this, Cogburn takes exception and growls back, "Fill your hands you son of a bitch." Untouched, unedited, his original retort and the scene are magnificent.

Cogburn takes his horse's reins in his teeth, clutches a Winchester carbine in each hand and rides down upon them. In turn, they charge him.

Try as they might, movie makers just can't get that kind of presence, that kind of machismo out of a Hollywood car chase.

There are a lot of movies out there. New ones being made every day. Few, if any, are Westerns. There just doesn't seem to be a market for Westerns anymore. They're too passe for the fast, over-complicated times in which we live. Many of the new modern-day movies have more twists and turns than a Busch Gardens rollercoaster. Sometimes, that's okay.

But sometimes we need a break from complexity in our lives and in our movies. Sometimes we need to kick back and get back to basics, back to simpler times. Times when we "grown up boys" were truly boys, blasting away with a pair of toy Roy Rogers six-guns.

At the end of True Grit, John Wayne as Rooster Cogburn bids goodbye to the young woman he has befriended and rescued. He good-naturedly invites her to "Come see a fat old man some time." With that, and a wave of his hat, he spurs his horse into action, jumps a four-rail fence, and rides off at a hard gallop.

Magnificent. Simply magnificent.

PART 3
SOCIAL STUDIES

FIFTEEN
MALE BATHROOM FAUX PAWS

As unsolicited greetings in public bathrooms go, the man sounded just a bit too enthusiastic to see me. For a moment, I was prepared to assume the habitually televised Kung Fu lotus position in the belief that I might have to do terrible things to his Adam's apple.

But for the moment, I restrained myself, nodding and smiling politely, as I began washing my hands in the remaining sink next to him. Rapidly.

From the corner of my eye, I could see that he was probably in his mid-fifties, with a gray flat-top, clean-cut, nicely dressed, pleasant in appearance.

"I'm just glad to see another gentleman come in here, he explained necessarily, as he continued washing his hands. "I wonder how many of these other guys would get dances from the ladies out there if the ladies knew they didn't wash their hands after they went to the bathroom."

Sure enough, while drying my hands, I watched about ten guys depart the nightclub's men's room without so much as even glancing in the direction of the bathroom sinks.

In fact, aside from my new—found gentleman friend, and myself, there were no other hygienically-correct guys departing the men's room.

Unfortunately, I've since observed that this unsanitary practice seems to be being followed by multitudes of the male population who have sought relief in public restrooms.

Years ago, I can recall that on a particular TV series the male main character had just finished washing his hands in a men's room when he was offered a handshake by a man who had just found relief and had not washed his hands.

Understandably, the gentlemanly main character ignored the man's soiled, offered hand.

I know that I certainly do not wish to shake the unwashed hand of a man who has handled his "quigley". And, like my older, flat-topped, gentleman friend, I just can't see women approving of such a flagrant male hygienic faux paw.

Speaking of paws, guy hygienic violators take note:

next time you find relief in a bathroom, how about washing your hands, and join the rest of us gentlemanly guys who are both legally and hygienically, truly "peed off"!

SIXTEEN
CARDING FOR CALORIES

The Surgeon General has determined that tobacco smoking is not particularly conducive to good health.

The U.S. Congress has determined through intense study and selfless personal experimentation, that excessive consumption of alcoholic beverages is not particularly conducive to good health. Especially theirs, if they get caught!

The National Lawn Chair Association has determined that our excessive overeating is not particularly conducive to lawn chairs' good health.

But just how are the tolls of these vices measured upon the human body — aside from gray teeth, beer bellies, and chiropractic bills?

The effects of tobacco smoking are determined by a "photo opportunity" involving an X—ray machine and a learned physician.

The effects of alcohol consumption are measured by a roadside test, usually conducted by an unsummoned, yet accommodating, officer of the law.

The effects of excessive overeating do not require the use of an X-ray machine or an officer of the law to be observed. They merely require a pair of moderately operative

"peepers" with which to observe two principle characteristics: 1. the presence of overly disproportionate portions of a Jello-like mass about one's midriff area; and 2. a trail of devastation: mangled heaps of aluminum tubing and gnarled lawn chair strapping dotting the patios and pool decks of Mr. and Mrs. America.

"Excessive overeaters" does not refer to persons who simply have a problem pushing themselves away from the breakfast table, or the brunch table, or the lunch table, or the dinner table, or the supper table, or the snack table, or the restaurant table, or the kitchen table, or the ever—popular dining room table, but to people who, if given the opportunity, would finish their meal and would then eat the table. Excessive overeaters refers to persons who appear as if they have escaped from the Largest Living Mammal Exhibit at Sea World.

As is the case with most serious disorders, there are usually signs to warn excessive overeaters of an impending condition. Having to turn sideways in order to fit through doorways might be one clue. Perhaps their appearing outside the front door of Doug' s All You Can Eat Smorgasbord and

Doug locking the door in their face and immediately beginning piling up large pieces of furniture against the door, might be another.

For years, the manufacturers of "Special K" breakfast cereal offered a simple, yet annoying preliminary self-test by which we are all challenged to expose a portion of our flesh in the vicinity of our waist as we attempt to "pinch an inch" of our own chubbiness between our thumb and forefinger.

The cereal self-test rule of thumb (and forefinger) states that if we can obtain more than an inch of chubbiness between our fingers, we fail the test. Ninety-nine and one half per cent of the population of the United States fails the pinch test. The other one half of one per cent of the population who register an inch or less of fat, being a clan of jade green Gumby's with high metabolisms, living somewhere in the dense underbrush of the Pacific Northwest.

Of course, in these high-tech times body fat measured via a simple pinch between thumb and forefinger is not acceptable. Unless one's taking a pinch of dip or snuff.

From the Special K pinch, the first actual instrument which was used to measure body fat was a pair of barbeque grill burger-flipping tongs. The historic innovation occurred during a backyard cookout when Chubby "Chowdown" Frankfurter leaned just a little too close to the inebriated chef's sizzling steaks. After which the fired-up chef offered to "filet Chubby's mignon".

So historically, and in the interest of simplicity, we know that a pair of tongs will do the job. A large pair of tongs of the barbeque tool variety, with inches numbered in increments in black magic marker along the 20-inch handles. Some of us, however, me included, would be best serviced by an extra wide pair of Tongs with a double clutch for extra wide portions.

In the meantime, what of "Enos Enormous", case study, and male person of gargantuan proportions who thinks nothing of placing an order for himself for 4 servings of deep-dish lasagna in an Italian restaurant on a regular basis? He has the money. He will get what he orders. It is all perfectly legal. Currently.

Waiters and other appropriate restaurant workers must be given the legal authority to confront a person such as Mr. Enormous while placing his order for four servings of deep dish lasagna, three baskets of dinner rolls, and five ten-inch apple pies a la mode for his dessert, all the while salivating, and rolling the weighted emphasis of his double-wide derriere from his right cheek, to his left cheek, and so, from his right chair to his left chair in the anticipated glee of the arrival of his food.

After the waiter has documented Enormous' "Italian Banquet for One" on his ordering pad, without hesitation he should yank up the front, lower portion of Enormous' gargantuan shirt, "Tong him", and then announce that he will only be able to serve him a moderate portion of a strained fruit salad.

At that point, if Enormous resists, he should be read his rights and then be "a la carted" off to "Dieter's Prison" where he will be made to wear ridiculously short shorts, a midriff-baring tank top, and be subjected 24/7 to defcon three exercise videos such as "High Steppin'with Larry Large".

He will be coerced into drastically reforming his dietary habits while subsisting upon a diet of a combination of water and granulated shake mix (chocolate-flavored beach sand), hereto referred to as "Slimming Real Quick", which is a modern-day version of synthetic canned mud.

Certainly, it would take his appetite away. It would also seal a radiator leak in a '57 Buick.

We are all "Big People" here. I mean "Adults", though granted, some of us are both. The fact that we are adults has enabled most of us to legally acquire driver's licenses which enable us to drive motor vehicles which bring even the most distant D.Q. (Dairy Queen) promptly within reach.

Unlike the purchases of cigarettes and beer, salespersons in D.Q.'s and D.Q.-type establishments will sell ice cream to a person of any age and of any proportion. Further, the Federal Division of Alcohol, Tobacco, Firearms, and Ice Cream does not even have funding enough to efficiently police the distribution of this most blatant weight-offending substance and its calorie-infested cohorts such as cake, candy, and the like.

Let's examine the facts: We (the people) have determined that we will protect certain persons from the effects of cigarette smoking and alcohol for their own good, by not allowing those persons to purchase those two items until they "have achieved responsibility" by reaching a certain chronological line, i.e. age, drawn by state legislatures.

The chronological line is enforced by the presentation of the ever-popular photo ID card (i.e. a driver's license or a facsimile thereof) per a cashier's request in what the cashier determines to be chronologically questionable circumstances.

But aside from a chronological line, let us draw another line of sorts … a rotund one.

Let us say that young, semi-attractive, cashier Julie Loon is stationed behind her cash register at the corner supermarket. She has no customers until a man who appears as if he has swallowed a 1966 Volkswagen waddles up to her register pushing an overstuffed shopping cart.

Upon closer examination, we realize that our subject is none other than Enos Enormous, reoccurring case study, and restaurant pinup boy.

Enormous reaches into the mountainous pile of the selected grocery ensemble in his cart and begins to set several large, consumable items atop the cash register counter's mechanized treadmill. His selection includes fourteen large frozen deluxe pizzas, six boxes of fudgesicles, and six gallons of Birthday Cake Ice Cream. The latter containing enough grams of sugar and sweetness to suck the filings right out of your teeth.

By his selection, we reach two immediate conclusions: 1. These are items of contraband for a person of our subject's proportions; and 2. He must have a walk-in freezer at home.

Cashier: "Sir, I 'll need to see an I.D. with that."

Enormous : "What do you mean? "

Cashier: "I'm sorry, sir. You know the law. I will need to see an I.D. please."

Enormous: "Okay. Okay," he says, pulling out his wallet and tossing his driver's license onto the counter.

Cashier: "Sir, this I.D. says you weigh 150 pounds.

Enormous: "So?!" he responds nastily, nervously tearing into a bag of Nacho Cheese Doritos and beginning to "inhale" its contents.

Cashier: "Sir, this license is six years old. Mind stepping on the scale behind you, please ?!

Enormous: "Look," he says, forcing a smile. Just let me buy the stuff this once, okay? I promise I'll start a diet next week."

Cashier: "I'm sorry , sir. Up on the scale, please."

Enormous complies. Lights flash. Bells and buzzers sound.

Cashier: "Sir, with your current weight, the only items the computer will allow you to purchase is the can of nutmeg and the box of low-cal Brillo pads.

Enormous: "But what about my copy of "Just Desserts" magazine?"

Cashier: "Sorry, sir. Too many calories."

So let us "save a lawn chair (or two!) and let us join the National Lawn Chair Association in their call for federal legislation to be passed for the good of those huge citizens in our midst who are akin in size to Enos Enormous – those citizens who are attempting to redefine "The Big Bang Theory" as we know it.

SEVENTEEN
INFLATIONARY MEASURES

A national obsession for Mammoth Mammaries has "Busted Out" all over this country. Fortunately, most of the persons attempting to increase their natural, God-Given Breast-Budget Allotment are women. For the most part.

Many women who seek the enlargement of their Bosom Buddies do so in order to make themselves more attractive to members of the opposite sex.

The cleavaged "Silicone Valley" of the past has yielded to a "Saline Solution" of the future. A type of Saline Solution not necessarily found in the repertoire of modern-day contact lens wearers.

If "Personal Growth" is not a goal of a woman's already exceedingly-prominent, paired, anatomical inventory, then perhaps a reduction option might be a consideration.

Inflation. Deflation. Consideration. When it comes to their chested-choices, women seem to have more options than the U.S. economy.

Men are not that fortunate. The truth is, when it comes to their own chests, it is hard for men to acknowledge that anatomically, in their natural, God-Given state that many male chests have their shortcomings. Hard to acknowledge, because it is extremely difficult for any man to utilize the words "ANATOMICALLY" and "SHORTcomings" in the same sentence while describing their own body.

The reality is that many men remain secretly dissatisfied with the "pectoral projectory" of their own chests. The reason is women. Just as sure as the actors Al Pacino and Andy Garcia are the same person, women find men with "pronounced pec's" (pronounced "pecks") to be sexually alluring.

Despite many men's preference for women with busty bosoms, the reality is that beneath the white and blue collars of the U.S. male work-force mother nature has endowed very few men with anatomically prominent pec's.

The male "pec-ing order" may be defined as follows:

1. "Pec and Paw" - prominent pec's, just the kind many warm-blooded American females would like to get their hands (or "Paws") on; 2. "Pocket Protector Pec's" - flat, seemingly non-existent pec's whereby the most prominent, topographical chestal feature is a plastic, pen-filled, breast pocket protector; 3. "Pirate Pec's" - a set of pec's whereby the most prominent feature is a sunken chest.

Understandably, with all of these natural male chest maladies, some men will weaken. In many cases, male, pectoral implants are as close as the nearest plastic surgeon. Yet, any man who desires prominent pec's, and obtains them through surgical, synthetic means, without the sweat and strain of athletic endeavors is not a real man.

Just a boob.

EIGHTEEN
GOODBYE HI-GENE

I always hold doors open for other people, no matter their age, sex, creed, color, or political persuasion. Except for a recent incident, when I inadvertently failed to hold open a door while exiting a public rest room, regrettably inconveniencing a young father and his toddler-aged daughter.

My wife and I recently arrived at an area restaurant for our habitual Sunday post church lunch. Upon approaching the restaurant's entry door, I held the door open for my wife, while she entered, then I patiently remained holding the door open for an unaccompanied elderly lady who was alternately pushing and leaning on an aluminum walker, precariously shuffling toward the entryway as quickly as she could. She smiled and thanked me as she passed by, then thanked me again as I held open a second door for her which led into the actual restaurant.

Shortly after my wife and I were seated, and had ordered our food, I went to the men's bathroom to wash my hands. While washing my hands, I heard a child's voice as well as an adult's, coming from a nearby enclosed bathroom stall.

After drying my hands, I turned to leave, grasping the bathroom exit door handle with the wet paper towel I'd used to dry my hands. I pulled the bathroom door open, as I heard a toilet flush and the bathroom stall door swing open. I tossed the paper towel into the trash can on my way out and let the door swing closed behind me.

Much to my surprise, a young father and his impressionable, toddler aged daughter were on my heels and immediately pushed the door wide open right behind me, forgoing any semblance of a protective, bonding, mutual father daughter post potty, bacteria eliminating, hand washing session.

By pooh-poohing a hygienically and socially correct hand washing procedure, the young father and his innocent, unknowing little daughter, said goodbye to basic personal hygiene, and hello to Barry Bacteria and his disease prone pals.

As I rejoined my wife at our table, the young father and daughter seated themselves at a distant, large table, apparently rejoining four other children and three young, adult women.

When my wife returned from the salad bar, I excused myself in order to also partake in the restaurant's numerous bar laden, vegetative offerings. After picking up a plate and hastily contemplating the selection of leaf type for the foundation of my salad, I realized that the young father had stepped into line directly behind me, also wielding a chilled, yet hopefully barren, salad plate.

While I was thankful that he and his unwashed, bacteria-bearing hands were behind me, handling the cool, protruding, metal serving spoons after I did, I quickly discovered that he was a categorically aggressive buffeter. While his shiny black loafers appeared to be geographically positioned at somewhat of a respective, unencroaching distance behind me, the remainder of him appeared to be listing toward me at about a 45-degree angle, seemingly pushing me, apparently attempting to hurry me in my caloric journey along the assorted, garden fresh components of the restaurant's salad bar.

Once I had returned to the company of my wife at our table and the young father had returned to his family's table at the other end of the restaurant, I immediately began to graze upon the heaped, salad dressing topped, vegetative pyramid which I had carefully, yet had more than abundantly assembled from the chilled confines of the salad bar.

Shortly after my consummation of the salad, I observed the young, probably six year old boy, seated directly across from the hygienicallyerring young father, pull a serrated table knife to his face and noncha-lantly run his tongue along the blade, apparently completely oblivious to his father. Seemingly dissatisfied, the boy then inserted the knife's serrated blade deeply into his mouth, and slowly pulled it out, running his lips along either side of the blade as he did so.

Fortunately for the boy, the knife was not sharp. But then, neither was his daddy.

NINETEEN
NUTTIN TO IT

I threw away a couple million dollars the other day. It was easy. There was nothing to it.

The truly amazing thing was that it had nothing to do with a Lotto ticket or an envelope from Publisher's Clearing House. In actuality, it was a substantial chunk of a walnut shell.

Even though I recognized that a walnut shell was somewhat of a different message-bearing container than the more typically utilized envelope, I did not fail to realize the potential value of the message's contents.

It was the method of the message's delivery which I wasn't wild about. Yet, at worst, it was an unpleasant "oral communication".

On weekdays, those days officially recognized as "days of business", I force down oatmeal because it is allegedly good for me, although I would rather breakfast upon a fondued, wasabi-glazed gecko than eat the grainy gruel.

Per spousal agreement, weekends are mercifully oatmeal free. I devote those precious few weekend mornings to earnest attempts at stimulating the economy of the bakery fresh sugar cookie industry.

Gruel days (weekdays) for distraction, I habitually select a brand of gruel containing raisins, dates, and walnuts. I figure with the addition of a few variously textured accessories, it may somewhat distract me from thinking what I'm actually running down my neck.

One morning, while slurping my gruel, my bicuspids encountered a large, unlisted ingredient which seemed to be particularly defiant in sharing its chew-friendly properties.

After removing the shell fragment, I contemplated my brown, jagged find.

No doubt the legal weasels who appear with nauseating frequency on tacky, moral and ethic-less TV commercials begging for personal injury claims no matter their taint, would have loved to have shared in my find. Monetarily, of course.

All I'd have to do was pick up the phone and call the malodorously malicious, frequently televised law firm of Will Cheatem and Howe, and file a mental anguish lawsuit, claiming that I would never be able to eat another bowl of oatmeal for the rest of my life. Etc.

A scenario which I must admit was not without its attractiveness to me. Particularly the part about never eating oatmeal again.

Instead, I did the right thing. I chewed carefully and finished my oatmeal, chucked the wayward walnut shell chunk in the trash, and went on to work in order to accumulate money by the proud, old-fashioned way. By earning it.

Suing somebody or some company over an innocent, uninjurious mistake?

That'd just be nuts.

TWENTY
DISORDERLY EATING

While so called "Eating Disorders" have been basted with a great deal of attention lately, there has been starved little attention heaped upon that much more serious and much more widespread series of eating maladies commonly known as "Disorderly Eating".

Of course, Disorderly Eating does not refer to the actual willful, and so, alarming consumption of say, garlic-tainted, sidewalk-crawling crustaceans, or of allegedly healthful "toe-fu" (Oriental for "processed toe-jam") , or of gobbling down a wriggling succession of live sushi to the tune of "You've Never Been This Far Before" by Harry and the Halibuts at Bob's Live Bait, Sushi, And Tackle Shop.

In fact, many instances of Disorderly Eating actually occur during the afflicted person's "oral presentation", such as the following:

<u>Spotted Retriever Syndrome</u> - persons suffering from this disorder simply halt the forkful of caloric cargo several inches away from their quivering oral cavity, somewhere in the vicinity of say, Cleveland, and make their tastebud-spotted tongue go get it.

<u>The North Dakota Syndrome</u> (otherwise known as "The Far-Go, North Dakota Syndrome") - when making their oral presentation, persons suffering from this disorder simply by-pass their tongue, throat, and neighboring tonsils, in an attempt to unload their caloric cargo

somewhere in the vicinity of their spleen: just as FAR (as the fork will) GO.

Oral Robbers - these are persons who not only mail portions of their annual income to a religious P.O. Box in Tulsa, Oklahoma, they also have an apparent oral disorder which does not enable them to ever close their mouths properly while chewing food. The involuntary viewing of this procedure by co-diners often "Orally Robs" them of their appetites.

The Pink Carpet Treatment - rather than inserting forkfuls of gigged food into their mouths, persons suffering from this disorder actually give their entree "The Pink Carpet Treatment" by rolling their tongue out of their mouths, distributing the food onto it, and then rolling it back in.

Cuckoo Clock Syndrome - persons afflicted by this disorder perch their loaded forks a few inches away from their mouths, and then bob their heads forward, bird-like, latching their drawn, beak-like lips around the food, and then bob their heads backward, in order to swallow the caloric sustenance. Persons suffering from this syndrome are not only said to appear to "eat like a bird", they are also said to appear to be "Cuckoo".

International Raking Syndrome - as they withdraw their eating utensils from their toothed orifices, persons afflicted by this psychotic malady are obsessed with raking foreign-manufactured eating implements across their American teeth with an excruciatingly-audible "S-C-R-A-P-E!". After several years of practicing this affliction, many of these persons become nicknamed "Tine Teeth" for the resulting permanent enamel furrows in their teeth, whereas many of their regular, fellow diners become nicknamed "Insane" due to years of having to listen to the toothed, psychotic scrape.

Where—Wolf Syndrome - persons not necessarily motivated by appetite who WOLF down their food so quickly, that fellow diners ask "WHERE did it go?"

Aqua-Nots - Alarmingly, while consuming even the largest of meals, these persons refuse to drink even a single drop of water, or any other liquid refreshment until they have completed the meal in its entirety.

Forget the TV shows and the movies, <u>this</u> is vivid proof of aliens in our midst.

<u>Sectional Eaters -</u> these are persons who will not begin eating another portion of food on their plates until they have completely finished the other: i.e. they will not touch their mashed potatoes until they have completely finished their green beans. Forefathers of these persons invented those annoying, sectional dinner plates which are often used in high school cafeterias. Those plates where the different sections are always too large or too small, where the various portions always spill over into one another anyway.

In military jargon, persons afflicted with this malady are ready for another section. A "Section 8".

TWENTY-ONE
SPECIAL PEOPLE

When I was a little feller, my Momma taught me many things. One of the things she taught me was manners, and how to mind them. In those early days, she recognized my please's and thank you's with high praise, and my occasional, lazy lapses into rudeness with a prompt swat on the rump.

As Mom was always very considerate of the feelings and needs of other persons, I can state that I am truly a better adult because of those childhood swats on the rear.

Speaking of "rears", it is time to take a swat at a seemingly increasing number of drivers who are lapsing into a rhapsody of rudeness. These are motorized "special people"

who actually accelerate at red lights so they can cut over into your lane into the narrowing twelve-foot distance between your car, and what was fleetingly, the car in front of yours.

All causing you to slam on your brakes, narrowly avoiding an accident. All by a thoughtless rear whose very life, and yours, apparently hinges on their being one car length ahead of you. All without consequential thought or provocation. All without a signal indicator.

Certainly, reckless deeds such as this tempt us into directing such rude and dangerous persons back onto the route of courtesy and consid-eration with the helpful aim of our middle finger.

Of course, it is tempting for us to follow up our personalized "signal indicator" to these recklessly rude cretins by giving them a generous serving of a piece of mind, but their Momma already tried that.

What they really need is something which their Momma should have given them in greater proportion: several good swift swats to the rear.

TWENTY-TWO
ANGRY BIRDS

An angry young woman "gave me the bird" the other day. When I say she "gave me the bird", I do not refer to a parrot, nor a parakeet, nor to any other member of the potentially buffalo-winged, beer-batter-fried, feathered fowl variety.

The bird which she bestowed upon me was quite of a different "nature". In fact, for a single, fleetingly flattering moment, I was hopeful that she might be taking the time to personally and officially designate me as a potential "Numero Uno" amongst my peers.

Until I recognized the digit. That single, bared, vertically inclined, backhand-served, most uncomplimentary, most central of digits.

Ironically, my girlfriend and I were returning from a Sunday church service, discussing a "bird" of another sort, at the time of the crime.

Our bird of discussion happened to be of a late, plump, privileged chicken which would soon be leisurely languishing toward the heights of culinary perfection amongst the hickory flames of my backyard barbeque grill.

During our drive, while I was blathering on about my culinary abilities, the young woman's car rolled about four feet into our path from a residential side street. A slow, simple automotive indiscretion.

A gentle tug of the steering wheel by my silent, unruffled girlfriend, and the young woman's automotive faux pas was countered and was history.

However, as the young woman's protruding car was aimed at my side and was conveniently located within only a few feet of our passing vehicle, and as the woman was not in any way unattractive, I could not help but turn my head to look at her while I continued my verbal rambling culinary discourse.

Whereby the angry young woman apparently interpreted my observation of her and my culinary-based, clamoring jaws as a personal, possibly slanderous critique of her automotive skills, and thereby promptly and without hesitation certified me as "Numero Uno".

I do not fault the angry young woman for her erroneous conclusion.

We've all had bad days. Some of us, more than others.

Perhaps the young woman had been unfortunate enough to sample my actual chicken-cooking abilities at another venue and was taking the opportunity to express her earnest, somewhat belated opinion.

Yet, no matter her reasoning, next time, before angrily gesticulating her opinion, I would advise the woman to take a minute to consider the appropriate, pertinent philosophies of two great men: John Lennon, and Colonel Harland Sanders. All I am saying is give peace or at least piece, a chance.

TWENTY-THREE
BLOWING THE BURG

Not too long ago, I was standing in line at the grocery store. In line ahead of me was a young man who appeared to be in his early twenties, wearing a brown, antiqued-leather jacket. He was a talker.

The young female cashier politely feigned interest as she ran the UPC codes of his selected purchases over the cash register scanner.

"I've lived here a long time," the young man loudly chortled. "I'm originally from New York. Now, that was a happenin' place. Soon as I get some money together, I'm gonna blow this burg. Maybe I'll go out West to California. Maybe I'll move back up to New York."

My first instinct was to immediately abandon my selected grocery items upon the counter, and to delve deep within my pockets, and generously contribute every penny I had in order to hasten the young man's residential departure from our midst.

Not only do I adamantly adhere to the doctrine of "America: Love It or Leave It" I have heartily adapted the patriotic credo to include my hometown of Lakeland, as well.

I first visited Lakeland in 1956, when I was eleven months old. While I cannot honestly state that I can recall a great deal about that specific visit, I do have it on pretty good authority that I did drool a lot, and that I did manage to stagger forth my first few steps on this earth during that particular visit, while upon official Lakeland soil at my grandparents' house.

Despite my career Air Force father's repetitive requests throughout the years, to be stationed near Lakeland, or even within the State of Florida, we never made it.

No matter where Dad's Air Force career took us, every year we took two weeks off during the summer to visit Lakeland and my paternal grandparents, my aunt, uncle and our three cousins.

Lakeland has been the only true home we've ever known. As my brother and I grew up throughout the years, always spending a small portion of our summers in Lakeland, the city's natural beauty became a familiar, welcome part of our lives.

The brilliant sunshine, the beautiful, placid, sun-glimmering lakes which attractively mirrored and aquatically-dimpled the city. The quiet palm tree-lined residential streets which led up to, and respectively embraced the city's abundant lakes.

Lakeland holds many wonderful childhood memories, as well. Riding bikes, buying and trading baseball cards, fishing, feeding the ducks at Lake Morton and playing golf at Cleveland Heights Golf Course, my grandpa playing solitaire card games on the back porch, Grandma mischievously hiding her latest dress purchase from Grandpa. My brother and I climbing their backyard grapefruit tree, and the distinct, oft-heard cry of blue jays calling from their backyard.

Grandma and Grandpa are gone now. As is our beloved Lakeland aunt and uncle. But the rest of us are still here, carrying on the wonderfully-fortunate tradition of living in an All American City. A tradition of family values, of family, as well as living in a great place to raise one. A tradition of abundant natural beauty, of history, of friendships, and of caring. Good people. That's what Lakeland is all about.

The young man in the grocery store was just that: young. Often young people need or have to move away in order to gain a perspective of where they've been, or of where they're going, or of where they need to go. Sometimes even the not-so-young have to do the same. The bottom line here is love where you live" or move on. Find a place you love and live there.

As for me, I'm Lovin' Lakeland.

I'm also wondering if that "burg blowing" young man would accept a personal check.

PART 4
CHOW BABY!

TWENTY-FOUR
MILK OF AMNESIA

Unless I miss my guess, you are a mammal. And if you aren't, then you've probably already got your own reality TV show and had your mug splattered across the front page of the National Enquirer along with Laura Langostino, The Lobster-Headed Woman.

Time for a brief "Biology 101" flashback: the word

"mammal" is derived from the phrase "mammary glands" which produce milk by which the mammalian infant (i.e. me and most probably you) is fed.

Typically, milk is the first beverage to tickle our newly formed tonsils upon our debut into the world. My first beverage of choice - actually, my mother's, was a metallically-canned, blend of synthetic milk of circa mid-50's vintage from the Similac distillery. While I cannot quite recall the flavor of the infantile beverage, suffice it to say that it was a precursor to the adult beverages I consume today.

Back then, as soon as milk-mustachioed girls and boys had progressed to drinking our beverages from sippy cups, the milk merchandisers poured down upon us.

My first recollection of milk marketing was Elsie, the Borden spokescow. While Mr. Ed was a talking horse who had a TV show, Elsie was a cartooned talking cow who pitched milk to kids and parents via a series of TV commercials, milk cartons and milk trucks. Elsie had a motherly, pleasant, bovine face, benevolent horns, and a necklace made of over-sized daisy petals. Her TV commercial voice sounded as wholesome as the beverage she pitched.

While Elsie and her milk-producing cohorts pitched milk as a wholesome beverage which helped young'uns to develop strong bones and teeth, etc., in later years medical folks began raising awareness about a villainous, artery-clogging substance called cholesterol which could potentially be linked to the consumption of milk.

From there, things got a lot more complicated. The bovine beverage was diversified and distilled into a multitude of many different proofs and blends in order to appease the Cholesterol Patrol and to give consumers greater, allegedly more healthful choices. Some of these include:

"Half and Half" - a weak mixture for those persons who prefer their milk with a 50% portion of mixer.

"Cultured Buttermilk" - buttered milk with an artistic education.

"Skim Milk" - the only blend of "milk" which is legally approved by the Cholesterol Patrol. This "milk" is actually water with one un-heaping teaspoon of Coffee mate added.

"Pasteurized Milk" – milk flavored to the taste of the late milk connoisseur, Lou Pasteur.

"Non-Fat Dry Milk" – boxed Coffee mate.

"Homogenized Milk" – the official milk of the U.S. Gay Olympic Team.

"Acidophilus Milk" – a rare milk produced by a Greek Cow with indigestion.

"Evaporated Milk" – milk which does not exist. It's Evaporated.

TWENTY-FIVE
GOING TO JIMBO'S
ORIGINALLY PUBLISHED 1997, PORTIONS ADDED 2025

There is often a refreshing crispness in the air, this time of year. There is nothing quite like drawing in a breath of cool, fresh, invigorating winter air; unless of course, that cool, fresh, invigorating winter air has the delectable smoked scent of Jimbo's Pit Bar-B-Q wafting about within it.

No matter the time of year, this wonderful outdoor aromatic ambiance is always in season near the intersection of North Lake Parker Avenue and East Memorial Boulevard in Lakeland, Florida.

There is something special about Jimbo's during the holidays. It is a wonderful, restful, aromatic and culinary oasis during the hustling, bustling madness of the holiday season.

No matter where or when I am holiday shopping, I always have the good taste to find myself seated at Jimbo's, sipping a sweet, iced tea, watching the world go by.

The world seems to spin a bit slower when observed beneath the brow of the homey, red and white checked gingham valances atop Jimbo's windows. It just seems to make more sense.

During the holiday season folks often call weeks in advance to order their smoked turkey. Nearer the holidays, they swing by and pick them up. All smoked turkeys leave with a generous portion of Jimbo's taste-bud-tantalizing Bar-B-Q sauce.

Hundreds of hot, luscious, freshly baked apple pies are flying out of there, in tandem with the smoked turkeys. A white container of cider sauce in tow. A golden, gently tangy cider sauce which must be lazily trickled over the pale, flaky crust of each generous slice of the hot, fresh apple pie.

There is an amber ambiance to Jimbo's dining room. Layers upon layers of thick lacquer which has turned amber with age upon the sturdy pine members of the picnic-esque tables, pine bench seats and pine-planked walls and ceiling.

The dining room's decor is a reflection of the late owner Harold "Happy" Lehman's passion for antiques, the outdoors, and for the interesting. During the holiday season, Jimbo's is a very busy place. Lehman began as the business' manager when it opened on September 1, 1964, successfully buying it out and becoming sole owner a year later. He was one of the finest men I've ever known, often warmly greeting his customers by name as they entered the restaurant.

Since her father's passing in 2018, Harold's hardworking daughter Tracey continues to manage and to operate the restaurant, carrying on the sixty-year-old family tradition.

Artistic nature prints of cypress trees, of ducks, quail and turkey in the wild tastefully decorate the walls of the dining room.

A banjo, a ukulele, and a small guitar silently dangle along a side wall. Several large, permanently posed, largemouth bass, school upon the back wall. To the left of the fish, above the rear exit door leading to the bathroom's outback is an appropriate wooden deuce-seated sign reading "Ye Ole Out House".

Contemporary country music recordings dominate the musical listings on the working jukebox to the left of the back door. A couple of ancient, wooden, hand cranked telephones silently protrude from the wall above it.

The windowsill of the side wall which meets the jukebox corner is lined with old glass bottles and jugs of various colors, sizes and shapes.

The wall of the front corner at the bottles-end is plastered with plaques. Most of them wood. Some of them clocks. All of them pigs, in shape.

Dangling from a beam near the room's center post, near a pig windchime, is a large, clear, gallon-ous jar filled with hundreds of poultry wishbones.

The front windowsill is appropriately populated with a multitude of portly pigs, in various states and stages of pig repose. In fact, it might be said that Jimbo's prominent theme of decor is a celebration of the pig.

Certainly, their succulent, mouth-watering pork sandwich is the ultimate tribute to the curly-tailed critter.

Seated at Jimbo's, sipping on a sweet tea, while in the culinary accompaniment of a pork sandwich, sliced or chopped, depending upon my mood, a side of slaw, a side of "pups" (hush puppies) and a side of delectable barbeque beans, and I'm eating my favorite food at my favorite place in the world.

Of course, there's barbeque beef, and chicken, and ribs, and ham, and, for the more aquatically-oriented, a fried fish sandwich.

Jimbo's has been serving barbeque at the same locationfor sixty-one years. For the most part, through it all the Lehman's have had the good sense to keep the core menu and the appealing, overall décor the same.

I love that. Keeping Jimbo's, Jimbo's. Something and someone you can depend on. Can't say there's many people and places like that these days.

Speaking of décor, right about now I'm thinking of that big ole jar of wishbones. And I'm wishin'.

I'm wishin' I was at Jimbo's.

TWENTY-SIX
CHILI TODAY, HOT TAMALE

Sometimes a good bowl of chili can smell like a bad case of B.O. A powerfully pungent, malodorous, eye-watering, nose-running, spice-laden stench, pyrotechnically capable of snatching the very air from our lungs, only to later restore a wind to our sails of another sort.

We're talking a thick, volcanically smoldering, bean-mined, red meat-based, wet paper bag brown, nitrous roux. A make you cry to your mamma chili. Generously enhanced with a vast myriad of highly combustible culinary ingredients, potentially including jalapeno peppers, chili peppers, various allegedly potable pyro powders including chili powders, although often excluding gun powders, and a broad selection of wittily labeled, over the counter, bombastically high-octane liquid additives.

When it comes to chili, "regular", or "special" octane will not do. I've got to have premium, one hundred octane.

To my knowledge, I have loved chili all of my life, although I do not recall my Mom spoon-feeding me a version of Gerber's Chili, or even if they offered such a selection during my early, high-chair, crib-dwelling years. Although, I do not remember a whole lot about those years, except that I understand that I had more of an inclination for wearing my food, than I did for consuming it.

The first chili I remember eating was my mom's. It was homemade, delicious, somewhat soupy, and I suppose thankfully in those formative years, a bit low on octane. Basically, Mom's chili consisted of kidney beans, ground beef, canned tomatoes, and chili powder. It was one of my father's favorite meals. It also became one of mine.

The first chili I distinctively remember eating outside of home was at the golf course snack bar at Ramey Air Force Base, Puerto Rico, circa 1966 when I was eleven years old. Speedy served it to me. It cost about fifty cents. Speedy was a short, friendly, darkhaired, middle-aged Puerto Rican who cooked on the grill and manned the snack bar counter. He always wore a clean white, folded paper hat and a white apron. Although his English was somewhat limited, he certainly knew how to cook.

In between grilling delicious hamburgers, hot dogs, chili dogs and delving out generous bowls of tasty chili, Speedy happily popped the tops on many a can of cold beer for the multitude of thirsty golfers who frequented his snack bar. Speedy was renowned for his chili. My Dad and I loved it, as did a lot of the other golfers. It was less tomato-based and a bit more potent than my mom's. Although I did not realize it then, Speedy's chili was actually training chili for my young, developing taste buds.

Years later, after we'd left the base, and I'd gotten older and was less impressionable, Dad informed me that before we'd left, there had been rumors that Speedy's chili had actually been concocted and canned by a stateside, white poof-hatted, mustachioed chef named Boyardee. It didn't matter. My fond memory of those simpler times and of Speedy's chili is the personal gratification benchmark by which I measure all bowls of chili today.

Although my late father did not cook, he made an exception of chili. Toward middle age, Dad either concocted or found a recipe for premium chili. A homemade chili which our family tastefully reveres to this day. The most memorable, most appreciated ingredient of Dad's chili was the beef. Generous, hand-prepared chunks of quality, tender beef. He also included an ample quantity of beans, some mechanically altered (crushed) tomatoes, and just enough spiced culinary pyro power to light me up like a Christmas tree.

In short, regarding the potential consumption of seemingly malodorous chili, I would give the following advice to the aromatically-wavering chili novice: Get past the B.O. and go grab the Bean-O.

TWENTY-SEVEN
THE BEET GOES ON

As we get older, the aging process often leads us to a maturing personal growth. A maturing personal growth which directly affects our virtues, our values, our ethics, and of course, our waistlines.

Still another aspect of aging, somewhat related to the waistline factor is the natural, yet inexplicable, middle-aged re-generation of our taste buds, during which our aging taste buds have apparently become bored with the years and years of the repetitive tastes of our favorite foods and judiciously evolve into reconsidering foods which they (we) once hated.

Fact is, even in these tremulant and troubled times, we must be frugal about the implications of utilizing such a powerful word as "hate".

But I do know that I will always hate beets.

From my first recollection, I have always hated beets. As a child, it would have been in my best interest to make the crimson, putrid-tasting vegetables disappear from my dinner plate by slipping them to our family dog, as he greedily awaited handouts beneath the family dinner table, but I didn't, for fear that they would kill him.

I was pretty sure that they'd do the same to me. The way I saw it, it took courage not to eat them, courage to endure the lengthy, well-intentioned parental lectures addressing the "earthy" crimson fare. If I want to eat something "earthy", I'll reach down and pick up a handful of dirt, thank you very much.

Courage. Courage is what this article is all about. That, and personal (belt—size—type) growth. That, and hopefully a beet-tolerant, realignment of my taste buds.

Unfortunately, it might appear unfair, and perhaps even somewhat weak on my part if I were to attempt to reintroduce my middle-aged buds to only a single preparation of beets. I therefore bravely, and regretfully, selected a wide variety of the crimson vegetative fare.

The unwitting participants in my personal test of culinary courage included:

Grade A Fancy Cut Beets, Fresh Cut Sliced Beets, Whole Ruby Red Pickled Beets, SweetAnd Tangy Sliced Pickled Beets With Onions, and Microwave Ready Ruby Red Sweet, and also, Sour Harvard Beets the latter, apparently Ruby Red Beets with a college education, as Mark Twain might have noted.

Before the first can of cut beets had completed the 360-degree revolution on the electric can opener, my nostrils filled with a dank, heavy odor. The contents of both cans of the cut (a.k.a. sliced) beets tasted like a cross between a soft, anemic red carrot, and a ration of sliced, solidified pencil shavings.

The pickled beets tasted like an experimental jar of wide, red, sweet gherkins gone awry, whereas the tangy sliced pickled beets with onions tasted like a bad batch of onion juice cluttered with sliced crimson vegetable carnage.

The alleged Ruby Red Sweet and Sour Harvard Beets may have been "Microwave Ready", but I wasn't.

I still hate beets.

Even us Beet-Haters must realize that despite our distaste for beets, "The Beet Goes On". So, the next time we're offered beets, we must try to keep our disposition SUNNY, AND by all means, SHARE!

TWENTY-EIGHT
GOING NUTS

Let us consider for a moment the culinary origin of that most landlocked, that most un-aquatic, of oysters: "The Mountain Oyster".

At just what point did the maniacally disturbed, Crisco-ed Cojones-dining,

Moonshine-swilling, culinary-pioneering goober initially declare: "Earl, ya know what I believe I got a taste for?"

I guarantee you, Earl ain't stopped runnin' yet.

Yet, the disturbingly "snippy", culinary psychotic tradition of dining on Mountain Oysters continues, even today.

Just what the Sam Hill are these people thinking?! They either don't quite have the minimal regulation number of required forks in their family tree, or they're representing disgruntled wives as over-zealous divorce lawyers, which by most counts means that by law and by nature, that they have an inherent and natural tendency to go for a male's "M&M's" (a.k.a. "Mountain Mollusks").

Over-zealous, would-be Mountain Oyster Shucking divorce lawyers aside, it is one thing to contribute to the breed-bridling conversion of particularly unlucky (in fact, never to "get lucky" again) male critters from "stereo" to "steereo"; it is quite another to dine upon the "paired proceeds" rendered by the occasion (i.e. remnants of the "alteration altercation").

Good Gawd people! Of all the latitudes and of all the longitudes; of all the gin joints and of all the juke joints in all the world; of all the offerings between the Soup of the Day and Cheddar Cheesecake, why do such demented culinary culprits insist upon routing their forks "Below the Paternal Equinox" (a.k.a. "dining below the belt")?

In the 1988 movie "Funny Farm" starring Chevy Chase as urbanite turned ruralite Andy Farmer, Chase is seated at the counter of a Vermont country diner, enthusiastically scarfing down a local, vaguely-defined dish of "Lamb fries", which appears to be composed of a glistening compilation of meatballs.

The admiringly-supportive, combination cook and waitress behind the counter stand posed to change the previously chalk-tallied record for consuming the apparently taste tantalizing spheres, and promptly do so, as Chase spiritedly rallies to the culinary cause.

After Chase pops number 30 into his mouth, the woman behind the counter matter-of-factly remarks, "I thought that record was gonna last forever. Most folks just don't seem to have a taste for testicles no more."

Chase's bug-eyed face freezes in horror, then spasmodically puckers, as the last post-record-breaking sphere he gobbled, blasts outward, punctuating his frantic, ill-stricken departure from the diner, after which an apparently testicularly-enthused local male co-diner delves into the remainder of Chase's abandoned culinary fare.

While Chase's violent reaction to ingesting the "sphered fare" should be considered a normal one for the majority of the American population, if habitual Mountain Oyster consumers' dining inclinations are challenged, by most counts, they can become more than a bit teste.

Yet, metaphorically speaking, the controversial dish and the related issues are balls which are better left in someone else's court. Preferably someone whose court is located far, far, away. Like say, Vermont.

TWENTY-NINE

WHAT'S AT STEAK WITH POTTED MEAT? (1997)

Recently, a close personal friend of mine remarked that as a child, her parents had served overly generous portions of "Potted Meat" at the family dinner table.

While I had never heard of anyone who had ever served "Potted Meat" before, I had heard of people who had served "Potted Plants" before. In fact, I once served five to ten for possession of some of my very own Potted Plants during the 1970's.

Yet, Potted Meat was an alleged organic substance whose culinary properties and values I had never explored, until I recently purchased a three ounce can of enticingly labeled "Potted Meat Food Product" from my grocer's shelf.

In doing so, I discovered that Potted Meat does not come in pots. Also, for any still hallucinogenically-adventurous children of the 60's and 70's, Potted Meat does not have any "interesting side effects". In fact, the only side effect that I experienced was a bit of a gagging sensation, occurring immediately after reading the product's list of ingredients.

Potted Meat is trite with tripe. "Beef Tripe". It also contains "Partially Defatted Cooked Pork Fatty Tissue, Beef Hearts, Partially

Defatted Cooked Beef Fatty Tissue", and my personal favorite, "Mechanically Separated Chicken".

In texture, I found the presentation to be somewhat of a pink, meaty paste, not unlike the consistency of a comparably sized can of Elmer's Wood Putty.

As far as flavor, I'm certain that I would have preferred that of the Elmer's Wood Putty, had a can of that product been readily available at the time.

Yet, a thorough investigation of Potted Meat cannot stop after only examining the nominative nemesis of the culinary category. We must "Press On", ('Squeeze and turn in the direction of arrow') courtesy of my manual can opener.

In returning to the grocery store, and in locating the products which were most similar to that of Potted Meat, I came upon a product fitting the Potted Meat criteria called "Friskies Alpo, Chunky Meat With Beef". While the ingredients listing was more appetizing, i.e. "Meat By Products, Chicken, Beef, etc., than the "Potted Meat Food Product" had been, I could not help but notice that the label advertised "Now! More Nutritious!". That's important to look for when selecting a can of Potted Meat. And, unusual.

I found the texture of the Friskies Alpo to be soft, yet chunky, with a taste which shouted "Beef!", yet whispered "Cereal". "Sheba with Tender Beef in Meat Juices" label not only boasted the most meaty variety of the taste test products: "Beef By-Products, Meat By-Products, Liver, and Poultry By-Products, etc." It was also the tastiest, although I am not personally partial to organ meat.

"Roast Beef Hash" was infested with tiny, squared potatoes, and was the most boring of the Potted Meat products tested. It needed a little something. Like flavor. Or possibly, the culinary accompaniment of some scrambled eggs, hash browns, and a side of grits.

Speaking of grits, our next canned subject contained "Soy Grits" amongst its nutritional regimen. As advertised, "Ken-L Ration Premium, Hearty Chunks in Gravy with Beef" was indeed, hearty with beef. I found the chunks to be a bit chewy, though beefy in flavor, with an imposing, yet nutritional hint of fibered cereal.

I had to try "Pedigree, Beef and Liver Dinner In Meaty Juices" because once in a while I just like to spoil myself. "Pedigree" says it all. The name alone makes you feel like a breed above the rest.

I found Pedigree to be very similar to the texture of the "Roast Beef Hash", only it didn't have those little squared potatoes. Also, Pedigree surpassed the Hash in flavor, because it had some.

The final Potted Meat product which I investigated was "Spam". What more can be said about Spam that hasn't already been said? It has been around for eons. For just about as long, it has been advertised on baseball caps, T-shirts, TV, and racing cars. We still don't know what it is. Although we do know that it is solidified, ready-to-slice Potted Meat.

Spam's mysterious ingredients are listed as "Pork with Ham", and of course, "Mechanically Separated Chicken Parts".

Yet, I thought Pork WAS Ham, and Ham WAS Pork. I'm confused.

If, after reading this, you find yourself craving a taste for Potted Meat, YOU are confused! Seek professional help, immediately!

If you must have something Potted, go with plants. Just be very careful of the specific types of plants you go with. Or else you might spend five to ten in the County Pen.

PART 5
GETTING OLDER

THIRTY
MALE HAIR MIGRATION

As men age, their hair care product needs may evolve from Vitalis Hair Tonic to Simonize Paste Wax. This is because their *hair care needs* have morphed into their *head care needs*. This is because their hairlines have receded all the way back to Milwaukee, Wisconsin.

As a result, some men find it necessary to pay exorbitant sums in order to purchase miniature "area rugs" resembling squashed, dye-tinted, Lhasa Apso's in order to disguise their natural, cranial defoliation. Most of these men profess to believe that sporting such artificial turf enables them to be more attractive to women. Yet, many women do not always find this to be the case. Particularly, those owning Lhasa Apso's.

As long as a man has hair a woman can run her fingers through, a woman can find follicular fulfillment in a man. So, if a man does not have an adequate crop atop his noggin, then he'd better have an abundant batch upon his chest.

In short, why should a woman fool around with a "throw rug" when she can have "wall-to-wall? Wall-to-wall chest hair on a man, that is. Women will even forgive a man's lack of muscular chest development, as long as his follicular chest foliage is *dense* and *lush* - two adjectives which hopefully do not also describe two aspects of the man's personality.

While not all men's heads of hair, or a male-patterned lack thereof, are the same, neither is the distribution of their chest hair features. Documented male chestal follicular formations include:

The Mr. T - a perpendicular formation, originating from breast to breast, then narrowly descending to the belly button, distinctly exhibiting a "T" shape. Bearers of this follicular formation tend to wear a lot of gold jewelry, occasionally mohawk hairdos, and watch a lot of reruns of 1980's action/adventure TV shows.

The Mr. T-Back - same as the Mr. T, only originating from shoulder blade to shoulder blade, and then, narrowly descending the middle of the back: something we really don't want to see. Possible solutions: 1. A good razor; or 2. a tv channel selector.

The David "The Poodle" Hasselhoff - an unnatural, overabundance of male chest hair on the human body. Bearers of this formation can often be found topless, running up and down beaches for no apparent reason while carrying personal flotation devices.

The Gomer Pile - A follicular formation of the chest whereby the most prominent follicular feature is the hair atop the guy's head. Even if he's bald. Bearers of this formation (or lack, thereof) are given to inexplicably bursting into baritone operatic song; also, they are not only Presidents of The Chest Hair Club for Men, they are also clients.

THIRTY-ONE
TUMMY TROUBLE

There are certain days when we middle-aged guys just "have it". Days when we can simply strut our mature, possibly less-than-perfect, middle-aged bods and turn the heads and radiate smiles from even the most voluptuous of babes.

Of course, these incidents primarily occur on days when we have absentmindedly failed to run our trousers fly completely "up the flagpole".

For some men, reaching middle-age can be like a downhill ride in a bakery truck. It is that time in a man's life when his personal anatomical inventory of "baked goods" becomes dated, losing its originally-packaged-freshness, whereby what was once "Beefcake" becomes "Moon Pie".

Consequently, middle-age can also be that time in a man's life when he can easily develop "tummy trouble". By "tummy trouble", I do not refer to a recurrent, tumultuous condition resulting from decades of bombastic culinary intake, which is routinely extinguished by that often repeated, TV-prescribed remedy; "My doctor said Mylanta".

The "tummy trouble" to which I'm referring is that middle-aged male condition in which some of us may appear to have swallowed a regulation-sized beachball.

Frankly, middle-age is that time in a man's life when he must realize that the potential promise of a "Middle-aged Spread" is not necessarily defined as a forty-acre parcel of farmland in Butte, Montana.

It's that time in a man's life when the "washboard stomach" of his youth has agitated downward, into the "spin cycle" of life.

While women have cleverly-designed clothing devices with which to rein-in anatomical protrusions, such as girdles, control-top panty hose, and apricot-colored brassieres, men only have polyester-belted Sansabelt Slacks, velcro cummerbunds, and their version of "braziers" which is an ice cream selection, available local Dairy Queens.

Aside from oversized middle-aged male tee-shirt Moo—Moo's sported with saltwater gamefish illustrations, amazingly, another portion of middle-aged-friendly male attire is the belt.

No matter how great the expansion of a middle-aged man's tummy terrain, his belt size never increases. This is because as a man ages, his waist relocates to a lower latitude. While this middle-aged male phenomenon can save him a fortune in new belt purchases every year, there can be serious side effects.

For instance, if necessity requires the belt to be lowered and buckled in the area of the kneecaps in order to avoid the projection of a pronounced paunch and the purchase of a larger-sized belt, he's doing it.

Tummy-plus-sized middle-aged men can take pride in that there have been a number of Prominent Paunches: There was Paunch De Leon, that famous, overweight, middle-aged Spaniard who spent the majority of his adult life in the state of Florida in 80-90 degree temperatures while attired in a trendy, helmeted, Revere Ware suit, while vainly searching for an elusive, legendary fountain of Chocolate-flavored Slimming Real Quick.

There was Paunch-o who starred as the sidekick of The Crisco Kid on the old Western TV series of the same name. The Crisco Kid and Paunch-o spent their lives traveling throughout the old West, while they gobbled down chicken deep-fried in Crisco oil, and listened to Loretta Lynn records.

There was Paunch-o Villa, that well-rounded bandit of Mexican fame who had visibly made one too many burrito "runs for the border".

Villa would one day have a distant American descendant named "Bob" who would drop one of the "l's" in Villa, overly-enunciate the other, and would make a living watching a Yankee carpenter named Norm renovate "These Old Houses" on national television.

As for me, my doctor said 'Mylanta'.

THIRTY-TWO
REMEMBER THE MANE!

If given the choice of shopping with the wife for a new set of percale bed sheets with a 270 thread count or watching the playoff game, ninety-nine per cent of the men are opting for the game. This what is known as a PATTERN. It is a documented, hereditary fact that some MALE PATTERNS can lead to defoliation of their noggins. In short, to Male Pattern Baldness.

As we age, many of us guys look into the bathroom mirror each morning, only to see that we have less hair to trim and more face to wash.

But we partially or completely cranially-defoliated men must take heart and recognize of all God's creatures, a BALD eagle was the hairless creature our founding fathers selected to be the powerful, patriotic symbol of these United States. So, bald is a symbol of strength, power, and courage. And hopefully good for at least a twenty-percent discount on a haircut at a barber shop of your choice.

While the hairline is the frontline of the fragile fringe of the male aging process, we must recognize and identify three distinct major pattern types of male hairlines in retreat:

1. The Divot Look - an appearance familiar to, but not exclusive of, male golfers; the frontal portion of the scalp is barren, except for a small,

isolated patch of courageous, remaining hair, which despite its origin, has the appearance of a piece of vegetative turf which has been whomped out of the fairway after a successful golf shot, and is replanted upon a relatively vegetative—less plain.

2. The Bald Tire Look (a.k.a. "On the rim and out the door") - an appearance whereby subject's hair has retreated to a final crescented crescendo around the rear lower rim of his head: from sideburn area, back around to the opposite sideburn area. Balancing and valve stems available at an additional charge.

3. The Telly Savalas Look - an appearance named after the late, multi-talented actor, whereby one's frontal hairline has retreated to the nape of one's neck; possible side effects: an inherent craving for lollipops, inquiring "Who loves ya, Baby?" to persons subject does not even know, and an inexplicable desire to watch old "Kojak" reruns.

There are, of course, alternative hairstyle options for men's defoliated noggins:

1. Toupee - a partial hairpiece, usually cemented down onto hair follicle clearings; can often resemble an electrocuted tarantula, or the business end of a recently deceased squid.
2. Raking - a method by which the subject parts his remaining hair a bit lower than normal, say at about the earlobe, combing his sparse, extended locks over the top of his otherwise bald head, giving the coifed, finished appearance of an artistically cultivated linguini patch.
3. Wall —To—Wall Carpeting — when a simple "rug" won't do; the most coverage per square yard available. Warning – the final, heavily hair sprayed arrangement can result in "Helmet Hair" . Please note that this helmet-like hairstyle has not yet been approved for use as an actual helmet in regulation play by any of the major football leagues.
4. Corn Row Treatment -— transplanting hairs from prosperous hair portions of subject's body, into carefully aligned rows along the scalp, somewhat like a human chia pet; Note: the stalks don't have any ears, but the sides of the subject's head often do.

5. Oodles Of Noodles — a treatment whereby the subject grows the six remaining hairs on his head to respective, minimum lengths of 87 feet and then distributes them over the extensively hair—parched area in serpentine fashion, somewhat like spaghetti over a cranium—shaped plate; Note: the addition of grated parmesan cheese is not recommended, as it may give the appearance of an infestation of dandruff.

6. Neanderthal Look — a method which takes advantage of sudden surges in the growth of male middle—aged body hair which always occur everywhere but on top of the head. In this method, the subject enhances and cultivates his overactive, continually sprouting eyebrows, until when combed backward, up onto his head his eyebrow hair easily covers a large portion of their hair-barren head.

While many of us middle-aged guys are alarmed about the retreat of our cranial crop, we must not panic. We must remember that simple lesson which we learned in high school geography class which is now in vogue: exposed topography is the coolest of all.

PART 6

BOTANICAL BUDS

THIRTY-THREE
FUN WITH PHIL (O. DENDRON) AND OKRA

Man and woman's first relationship with plants occurred with the "first couple". No, not the President and the First Lady of the United States, but with the original couple who had dibs on the very first address ever! Adam and Eve, P.O. Box 1, Garden of Eden.

Their first selection of attire was "in fig". Fig foliage, to be precise. It is fortunate that their "Botanical Boutique" in the Garden of Eden apparently did not include an abundance of poisons ivy, oak, and sumac, or they might have slowed the evolution of the fashion industry a thousand years. Let alone commencing to add some branches to the family tree.

From the simple barren fig leaf, our Botanical Fashion has progressed to grass hula skirts, straw hats, straw shoes, and to the more sophisticated weavings of the cotton plant. Nowadays plants are eaten, smoked, sniffed, counterfeited, worn for articles of clothing, utilized as indoor and outdoor decor and are used as medicine and barter throughout the world.

In furthering our botanical knowledge, we must recognize that "Botany 500" is not only a 4 credit course at the Junior College, but is also a clothing firm which supplied "wardrobe" to TV game show hosts during the 1970's.

In addition, we must realize that our possession of certain particularly potent plants is against the law. This unpleasant factor is compounded by the distasteful realitythat some plants actually eat meat — a substance of which (gulp) we humans rather predominantly consist.

And yet, we cannot help but rain down the most fertile of Accolades and tributes for our living, leafed friends of the Botanical World.

We have even taken their names as our own: "Rose", "Daisy", "Violet", "Dahlia", "Jasmine", "Heather","Holly", "Fern", and "Lettice" (as in "Lettice—Romaine", or as in"Lettice—Iceberg", or as in "Honeymoon Salad: Lettice—Alone"), to name a few.

We have even named streets after them: "Lilac Lane", "Cow—itch Vine Boulevard" (not to be confused with "Hollywood Vine Boulevard"), and "Butterwort Place".

We often utilize the Botanical Expression "as similar as two peas in a pod"which pushes us upward into the " seed syndrome". We refer to our human professional tennis stars as "seeds", We have also installed "flavor—enhancing" sesame seeds (actually tasteless—enhancing) onto the buns of hamburgers, bread, bagels, and the like. We eat sunflower seeds by the bagful. Cow pastures are "peppered" with healthy, fertilizer—enriched tomato plants due to the indigestible pugnacity of the tomato seed — an endless, living cycle of Botanical Tribute.

Aside from giving many plant names to our children, we have also "cross—pollinated" the nominal tribute to include certain members of the animal kingdom by naming several plants in honor of respective animal body parts:

"Crab's—eye", "Deer—tongue", "Dog—tongue", "Dog—toothed Velvet" "Hound's—Tongue", "Lizard's Tail", "Lobster Claw", "Lamb's Ears Orchid", and "Goat's Beard".

Many plant names reflect our human romanticism: "Love Apple", "Love Vine", "Love Charm", "Mistletoe" (if not in name, in application), "Passion Flower", "Passion Vine", "Love-in-a-Mist", the botanically shredded "Love Lies Bleeding", the moody "Touch-Me-Not", and the sentimental "Forget-Me-Not".

We have also wrought religion upon our Botanical friends:

"Monk's Hood Orchid", "Star Of Bethlehem", "Crown Of Thorns",

"Angel's Trumpets", "Angel's Wand", and the sinister "Devil's Potato" so sinister, that it is sometimes punctuated with an "e".

Like many living creatures, plants are susceptible to "worts" (a Botanical spelling of "warts"), and to actually being named after them: "Lawn Pennywort", "Milkwort", "Ragwort", "St. Peter's Wort", "St. John's Wort", "Leadworts", and the disgustingly graphic "Hairy Pipeworts".

There are, of course, certain plant names the very selection of which makes one curious as to the origin of the particular Botanical discoverer:

"Glandular—Skullcap" - discovered by a frustrated Botanist who really wished to be a cross between aNeurosurgeon and an Endocrinologist.

"Horse—Mints discovered by a jockey who had been spending a bit too much time around the horses.

"Long-Stalked Monkey's Flower" - discovered by a misguided, soon —to—be disappointed person who should have spent much less time "stalking" as evidenced by the unappreciative monkey's reaction when presented with the flower.

"Red-Bearded Tongue" - discovered in a mirror by a person who had attended a "Bloody Mary themed drink fest the previous evening.

"Shoe Buttons" and "Shoe Strings" - discovered by shoe entrepreneur Caleb Cobbler.

"Toadshade" - discovered by Mr. Toad, just after his wild ride.

"Rhododendron" - discovered by a woman who shortened her name, became a friend of Mary Tyler Moore, and got her own TV show.

"Dutchman's Breeches" - discovered by a pants—less man who was searching for a lost goldmine.

"Cow-licks" - a type of plant discovered by child actor "Alfalfa" of the old "Little Rascals" comedy series.

No study of Botany would be complete without containing a helpful Botanical glossary:

"Air Potato" -a vegetative version of "Air Guitar"

"Croton" – a plant which produces miniature, dried, bread cubes often used in salads.

"Avocado" -an alleged "fruit" which transitions into "guacamole" when run over with a lawnmower.

"American Cowslip" – a plant sometimes included in the manufacture of hot dogs.

"Alligator Bonnet" – an extremely rare form of hat wear utilized by acquarian lizards.

"Bleeding Heart" – often found in the far left hand portion of the meadow or flowerbed.

"Jasmine" – 1. Botanical for "Jazz, man"; 2. a request for music.

"Dwarf Paw Paw" – the 8th, Senior Dwarf.

"Elder Berries" - old berries which were "stomped" into wine by Elton John.

"Aloe" - a foreign greeting.

"Okra" - a plant that used to have a TV talk show.

"Parsley Haw" - named in honor of one half of the famous TV country comedy team of "Hee" and "Haw".

"Plumbago" — a well—traveled recreational vine (a Botanical "RV").

"Smartweeds" -cultivated weeds.

"Impatiens" -plants with attitudes.

"Golden Shower" – often found in the vicinity of fire hydrants.

"Periwinkles" – a distant, Botanical relation to TV Star Bullwinkle Moose.

"Oleander" – a poisonous, Botanical butter/oleo substitute.

"Jack-In-The-Pulpit" – as opposed to "Oral-In-The-Pulpit" – a plant from which the facsimile of the open palm of a human hand appears to be protruding outward from the center (pulpit).

"Carolina—All—Spice" - a Botanical men's cologne, the fragrance of which does not come from the sea.

"Solomon's Seal" — as opposed to "Solomon's Seal Act".

"Chincherinchee" - chim chim cheroo.

"Bearded Iris" a woman who had a job with a carnival until the day she decided to shave.

PART 7

FASHION AND CELEBRITY

THIRTY-FOUR
A STUDY IN DRAWERS

I learned about Manifest Destiny in high school history class. Manifest Destiny is where countries like our own U.S. of A. go around gobbling up all of the additionalproperty that they can, INCREASING THE SIZE, and so, theMIGHT, of that country.

I have managed to do this on a PERSONAL SCALE. In fact, I have been able to measure my success by just that: by my "PERSONAL SCALE". The one I keep in the bathroom.

I have gone around gobbling up "additional property" (i.e. foods, and stuff; i.e. "foodstuffs"), which has succeeded in INCREASING THE SIZE of my waist, though I don'tknow about my MIGHT. In fact, speaking of "MIGHT", you MIGHT pass me another round of those mashed potatoes.

This "personal expansion" program has forced me to make certain inquiries into the Black (Jean) Market. No matter whether the jeans are black, white, or a versional blue,certain persons insist on calling the denimed drawers "blue jeans".

Then there are those persons who refer to jeans as "dungarees". What is that? As a Multi-tax-paying, hygienically-correct American, I refuse to pull on any article of clothing the name of which originates from the word "dung".

The only jeans-factor of which we can be truly certain is that the inventor of the "Button-Fly" option was not a person who consumed beer on a regular basis.

Also, at least one major jean manufacturer insists on posting the wearer's WAIST SIZE upon a publicly permanent, posterior label for God and all the world to see. Why not just have them post labels upon some of the "Bigger Boy" and "Bigger Girl" sizes reading "Humongous"?

Then there's those confusing jean style identification numbers. They have more triple-digit ID numbers than the Boeing Aircraft Corporation. They have numbers representing regular fit, skinny fit, loose fit, droopy drawer fit, flared fit, boot cut, baggy fit, relaxed fit, wide load, ultra-wide legs, and clown fit, to name a few.

Despite the broad selection, it would appear that the man in the street – particularly the young man - currently prefers the "Pant Load/Droopy Drawers Look".

Pass on that, thank you very much.

Speaking of "history" and Manifest Destiny, next month we'll review the offered jeans selection back in the days of Wyatt Earp, Matt Dillon, and Bat Masterson.

Wait a minute Wyatt Earp, Matt Dillon, and Bat Masterson - that wouldn't be Manifest Destiny.

That would be "The Marshall Plan".

THIRTY-FIVE
BURT AND ME

In the summer of 1982, while living in West Palm Beach, I considered myself to be a 27-year-old, part-time screenplay writer with an annoying, unrelated, full-time job which monopolized much of my time.

While in retrospect, I'm quite certain about the part about being 27 years old, and the bit about the annoying, unrelated, full-time job, I cannot help but shake my head when I think of my naïve attempts to write and to sell screenplays.

One evening back then, while laboring at my real-life, full-time job, an equally bored young co-worker and myself began conversing about what we liked to do during our respective personal time.

When I mentioned the fact that I had just finished writing a screen-play, my co—worker stated that he happened to know motion picture star Burt Reynolds' cousin who worked at The Burt Reynolds Horse Ranch in nearby Jupiter.

My co-worker stated that if I would give him a copy of the screen-play, he would give it to Mr. Reynolds' cousin, who would in turn give it to Mr. Reynolds.

After promptly, yet somewhat hesitantly giving my co—worker the screenplay, I patiently waited a couple of months before asking him if Mr. Reynolds had yet seen the screenplay.

According to my co-worker, Mr. Reynolds' cousin did have it and was going to give it to Mr. Reynolds, but hadn't had a chance to, the last time Burt was in town.

Perfectly understandable. For months, it was the "perfectly understandable" answer which I received to every inquiry made to my co-worker.

After nearly a year of the same response, I finally became suspicious and drove to the nearby Burt Reynolds Ranch where I asked for Mr. Reynolds' cousin.

I found him at the ranch's Tack and Feed Store. He was a pleasant, clean cut young man, about my own age.

After apologizing for bothering him, I simply asked if he knew my co—worker, either by name, or by description.

"No. Why?" he inquired.

I gushed forth a brief account of the story.

"Tell you what," Mr. Reynolds' cousin replied when I 'd finished, "You get that screenplay back, and I'll see it gets onto Burt's desk."

His response blew me away. What a guy! What an incredible thing to say! And to do!

After a brief, one-sided, no questions-asked confrontation with my co-worker, I got the screenplay back the following day and gratefully gave it to Mr. Reynolds cousin.

True to his word, he put it on Burt's desk. A few days later, I received it in my mailbox, along with a pleasant, but brief, rejection letter from the head of Burt Reynolds Productions, stating in essence that Mr. Reynolds was booked for the next few years with movie projects, and was not reviewing any more material at that time.

Two years later, a buddy and I answered a call for movie extras at Durty Nelly's, a Fort Lauderdale bar where a segment of a new Burt Reynolds movie called "Stick" was being filmed.

Although we arrived about three hours early and were about 20th and 21st in line, by the time the movie folks announced that they were going to start letting people into the building one-by-one, the crowd had become a mob of a few thousand people which surged forward into one large mass.

Women screamed. Young men angrily yelled out for the mob to stop pushing. Finally, they did stop. Though by then all of us were imprisoned by the mass of people. Our hands and arms were pressed attention-like at our sides in ninety-degree heat. We were so pressed together that it was nearly impossible to even scratch our own noses if we'd needed to.

After half an hour, my buddy did the sensible thing and pushed his way out of the crowd and went back to the car.

About three hours after they'd started, I was finally led into the building. Exhausted, somewhat disoriented from the heat and the stress of the pressing crowd, dripping wet with sweat, I answered my first and last, casting call for a major motion picture.

After being led toward a blindingly brilliant light through the dimly lit bar, I was told to hold up a piece of paper with my name and phone number on it and to look at the camera.

With sweat-matted hair, I squinted in the direction of the blinding light and forced a big, feigned Hollywood smile.

I was then led a few steps forward where I suddenly realized that a man's hand was out, offered to me. I grabbed onto it with my right hand, and while giving it a firm shake, and looked into Burt Reynolds' face.

I couldn't believe it! I was shaking hands with Burt Reynolds, the former number one box office star in the world! I'd seen most, if not all, of his movies

Amused by my earnest surprise, he grinned back at me. "Hi Burt!" I managed to blather out through the spread of my large, unfeigned smile.

He looked at my name on the piece of paper and said "Drew, thanks a lot for waiting. I appreciate it."

"Hey! No problem, Burt! No problem at all!" I managed to enthusiastically burst out.

I could have told him how great I thought he and his movies were. I could have told him what a great guy his cousin was, and how he'd helped me out. I could have told him that I'd written a couple of screenplays. I could have told him anything.

Instead, I stood there dumbfounded and starstruck, continuing to silently shake the man's hand with a frozen, stupefied grin across my face.

Moments later, I was whisked away, leaving Hollywood, screenplays, starring roles, and regretfully, Burt Reynolds, behind.

PART 8
SPORTING GOODS

THIRTY-SIX
BOBBING FOR BUGS

It began in my childhood, as do most serious afflictions of the human mind.

If they had only allowed me to do it. But they did not. The fact that they had constantly told me not to do it made me want to do it all the more.

My first recollections of running were in short bursts through the furniture—strewn pathways of our family home. The parental standing command of the day was "No running in the house!".

Gradually, when I became old enough, I began attending school and transposed running in the house to running in the hallways of the school. My efforts were greeted with shouts of "No running in the halls!" by well—rehearscd, well-meaning school faculty members.

And now, several decades later, I have stopped running in the house. I have also stopped running at work (the adult version of attending school) as I was drawing too much attention to myself.

For the better part of the past year, I have been doing my part to wear out the asphalt pedestrian path around a lake near my home with the undersides of my track shoes. Now, one year and three pairs of shoes later, I can confidently report that the process of wearing out the asphalt is going to take a bit longer than I had first anticipated.

And so now, around dusk, I am out there, doing what I was told not to do by my parents and by the well-meaning educators in my life, in order to try and recapture some of my faded youth.

My feet pound the pavement. My legs ache. My arms pump forward and backward. My mouth gasps for air. My heart pounds and my head bobs with each thrust of my legs.

In the warmer months, my head bobs through small clouds of swarming bugs, inevitably resulting in unwelcome bug intake, causing me to choke and cough in a futile attempt to dislodge the little insectic Kamikazes.

Move over Wheaties, Breakfast of Champions; Bugs are pure protein, Breakfast of Amphibians!

THIRTY-SEVEN
CAN'T WE JUST CALL IT HORSE RIDING?
(AN EMBARRASSINGLY TRUTHFUL ACCOUNT OF UNHORSEMAN-LIKE CONDUCT)

Horse*back* riding. As opposed to what other portion of the horse? What other portion of the horse's anatomy would accommodate a large leather saddle and a puckered human posterior? A hoof? A leg? A neck?

Do we call it bicycle *seat* riding? Do we call it motorcycle seat riding? No. We do not. After all, these are our mechanical horses of the 21st century.

Can't we just call it horse riding?

Although I am not a veterinarian, I do consider myself somewhat proficient in regard to identifying the anatomical portions of a horse. I can earnestly state this as some particular friends of mine habitually compare me to a particular portion of the horse's anatomy on a semi-regular basis.

I have never owned a horse, but I have spent hundreds of dollars on their behalf - although I no longer have the worthless WIN tickets to prove it.

Aside from their unappreciative displays toward me at racetracks, my personal One-on-one encounters with the equine-esque creatures have also been less than stellar.

As a rule, horse riding is fine with me, as long as the horse is rigid, gentle, has an empty, fixed gaze, and grazes on quarters. This "quarter horse", if you will, was not found in herds or on ranges, but rather, was mechanically tethered in front of local K-Mart stores. It was the only breed of horse with which I was completely at ease. Yet, the mechanical horse, like K-Mart has apparently gone extinct.

Back then, there was also the live pony ride at the annual local carnival. Mom would give the old, gray-haired gypsy a dime and he would help me up into the saddle on the sad, brown and white pony's back. The gypsy would then lead the pony around in circles while Mom clicked the Instamatic, my little brother cried, and I threw up.

My next encounter of the equestrian kind occurred when I was twelve years old. Due to a preadolescent attack of testosterone and bad luck, I found myself mounted bareback upon a large brown horse named Cocoa in the middle of a sugarcane field in Puerto Rico.

With a great deal of kicking, slapping and a rather colorful trail of seasoned expletives, I managed to accost my uncooperative mount into an angry gallop.

Five minutes later, I involuntarily experienced an unhorsemanlike dismount at about sixty-three miles per hour. I bounced once or twice and came to a rest in a tangled heap, waiting to be trampled in a victory dance by Cocoa's jubilant hoofs. It did not happen.

Totally indifferent to my plight, riderless Cocoa continued to head for the horizon at a gallop. I have not seen him since. I commandeered a stalk of sugarcane and enlisted its assistance as a crutch. It was a long limp home.

I entertained myself along the way with fond thoughts of Cocoa ending up as perishable inventory in the company of special sauce, lettuce and cheese in a Puerto Rican fast food restaurant.

THIRTY-EIGHT
NEEDING A BIGGER BOAT

Old Hitler is a legend on Gasparilla Island. Locals and visitors alike claim to have seen the enormous, shadowy outline of the twenty-some-foot-long hammerhead shark lurking beneath the surface of Boca Grande Pass, just off the southern tip of the island.

Some tale spinners report the appearance of the huge, scarred, man-eating beast to be so overwhelmingly evil, that they dubbed him "Old Hitler". That, and the possibility that some of the more enthusiastic, potentially beer-fueled folks may have reported sighting just a hint of a snub-nosed mustache above his upper lip.

Despite the tales and the potential danger, Dad and I were very enthusiastic about our Boca Grande fishing trip. The drive from home had been pleasant and

uneventful, particularly if you did not take into account the moment the boat trailer had become detached from the car's trailer hitch, and the boat had attempted to pass us in the oncoming lane of traffic.

After arriving at Boca Grande, launching the boat, and getting underway, Dad and I broke out a couple of ham and cheese sandwiches on white bread, a couple of sodas, and proceeded to have breakfast. When we got out to The Pass, we found the water to be a bit choppy.

But there were plenty of other boats out there. Although they were much larger and much more seaworthy than our fourteen-foot, tri-hull, freshwater ski boat.

As our boat bounced around like a cork, Dad and I began to fish. We each attended a respective rod, while a third unattended rod with an old, onery, closed-face reel was positioned at the stern of the boat, baited with a large, malodorous chunk of fish.

It wasn't long before the heavy-duty line on that troublesome reel at the stern of the boat began screaming, the line madly plunging downward into the depths of the choppy waters of Boca Grande Pass.

Dad handed the rod to me, and I began to fight the extremely powerful, unyielding undersea beast. While I strained and fought the creature, I could not help but notice that the sea was growing increasingly choppy. I particularly noticed this when I observed Dad hanging over the side of the boat, "having his breakfast" all over again.

I fought the unseen beast for over an hour before managing to finally pull him up from the depths, and alongside the boat.

Dad and I peered down into the water alongside the boat and shouted out colorful nautical exclamations of surprise. While not a hammerhead, we were looking at a large, somewhat fatigued, very angry shark of an unknown species which was only about eight feet shy of being as long as our precariously bobbing boat.

In his adrenalin rush, Dad snatched up the gaff and inexplicably attempted to slam the large hook into the creature's rhinoceros-like hide in an attempt to secure his capture. The gaff's hook bounced off the shark and apparently really peed him off. The angry creature instantly dove downward, snapping the line and thankfully disappearing into the depths below.

When I expressed my disappointment at not being able to boat the lengthy shark, Dad did not miss a beat, "If you'd have managed to boat him, I'd have gone over the side."

PART 9

RIDES

THIRTY-NINE
DRIVING US CRAZY

"Driving is not a right, it's a privilege."

Who is the righteous bonehead who injected this profound statement of brilliance into our American mainstream?

He must have never had his over-priced, over-financed, vehicle cough to a halt somewhere in heavy traffic, or somewhere beyond the realm of civilization.

He must have never encountered rudeness on the road: drivers making turns in their autos, trucks, and motorcycles, without exhibiting turn signals. He must have never been tailgated by Chad, the Clearasil Poster Kid who's racing daddy's car with tunes ablast to the corner convenience store to pick up a pack of Marlboros. He must never have had a flat tire in the middle of nowhere or on the interstate, or had someone suddenly cross over four lanes of traffic only to cut in front of him, etc., etc.

It is recorded fact that a lot of people's personalities change when they get behind the wheel of a motor vehicle, that the vehicles figuratively become extensions of certain portions of human anatomy. I believe this to be true, for upon occasion, I have suggested that certain drivers ARE some of those portions, at rather extended levels of my voice range while in the blaring, musical accompaniment of my vehicle's horn.

Also, while there is a simple test which is conducted to determine whether the oil in a vehicle is a quart low, there is no test to determine if *the vehicle's driver* is a "quart low" or not.

When regular electronic vehicular signals fail, drivers can communicate to other drivers by a series of hand signals: left arm extended in a horizontal plane, designates a left turn. Left arm extended vertically downward, designates "slow" or "stop".

Any signals whereby a particular finger of either hand is prominently displayed should be considered uncomplimentary to the person in whose general direction the finger is pointed, lending new definition to the phrase "designated driver".

FORTY
MONTE AND ME

You do not legally own a car until you've pushed it.

Only a month after purchasing the new 1979 Chevrolet Monte Carlo, my legal ownership of the vehicle was officially consummated. Something in the gearshift had gone haywire, not allowing me to restart the car in a convenience store parking lot.

Roy had Trigger. Dale had Buttermilk. Pat had Nellybelle. For over 15 years and 145,000 miles, I had Monte.

Monte was the first new car I had ever purchased. Still is. He had a beautiful oyster—colored interior, that fleeting new car smell, a white vinyl top, and most importantly, a shiny black exterior.

I had wanted to own a black car ever since I was a kid, because Fenton Hardy, the detective father of The Hardy Boys owned one. In my youth, I avidly followed the boys' exciting adventures in The Hardy Boys books by Franklin W. Dixon.

While people's lives are measured in years from their "original date of manufacture", so too, are our automotive compatriots.

Also, like people, by their mere existence, our automotive friends are susceptible to acquiring physical scars. Monte was no different. There was that worn spot in the carpet where I always rested my left foot while driving with my right.

There were the white paint flecks on the right rear fender which Monte had acquired while I was painting my boat in a dumpy, but affordable, Fort Lauderdale marina.

There was that hideous dent at the top of the passenger's door which had stopped a vandal's steel pipe after it had shattered Monte's window.

Perhaps the best times Monte and I ever had together were the years we went fishing and crabbing at our own special place beneath a particular bridge in Palm Beach County.

Then, there were all the special people who had climbed aboard for a ride with Monte and me over the years. Friends all. Some of whom we would never see again.

I had spent most of my driving life peering outward at the world through Monte's windshield. Corny as it is, like the song says, yes, we'd seen sunshine, and we'd seen rain.

In the end, Monte's metal roof had deteriorated. It was leaking severely, leaving puddles of water on the back floor and soaking my driver's seat after a rain. His plastic interior was disintegrating, while his shiny black exterior luster had faded into a thin, dull, sparse film which had worn away in several places.

I had postponed the inevitable for years. Monte held too many memories for me to easily let go.

Finally, I drove Monte to a modest used car lot on the edge of town and sold him for a pittance of his worth to me.

In saying goodbye to Monte, I was reminded of the words of Clint Eastwood in the movie "The Outlaw Josey Wales" when he was paying homage to a loyal, departing, traveling companion: "I rode with him. I got no complaints."

FORTY-ONE
CHRISTINA

"Christine", Stephen King's tale of horror regarding a 1958 Plymouth Fury automobile, idles in comparison to my own automotive horror story involving a 1972 MG Midget which I named "Christina". They do not make Midgets anymore. Uncoincidentally, from what I understand, the British MG company which manufactured the problem-prone Midgets, went out of business in 1972.

I purchased Christina at a used car lot in 1974. I had recently entered college and was in need of a set of wheels. Christina was a sporty, blue-green 4-speed convertible.

The first suspicious incident which occurred with Christina was life-threatening, as were a number of my incidents involving the car. Several unsettling incidents later, I had to be physically restrained from attempting to perform an unscheduled "tune-up" upon Christina while wielding an eight-pound sledgehammer.

The very first incident occurred shortly after I purchased her. I had stopped the car at a traffic light at a busy intersection.

Suddenly, a speeding, seemingly-huge (in fact, actually mid-sized) car attempted to turn in front of us, skidded on some wet pavement, and T-Boned into Christina, caving in the two-inch-thick door which was all there was between me and that "Great Motor Vehicle Service Lounge in the Sky".

Fortunately, I saw the skidding car coming and threw myself as far over to the passenger's side as possible, escaping without injury, only to be subjected to greater automotive dangers in the weeks ahead.

Almost immediately after obtaining Christina, I noted that she appeared to be exhibiting a persistent series of electrical problems. When it would rain, I would have a tendency to turn on the three front windshield wipers, and they would have a tendency to not work.

The same would go for the headlights. When I tested them during the day, they worked great. Yet, often at night I'd be driving down the road, when suddenly, no headlights.

It got to where I kept a large bag of assorted automotive fuses in the glove box, in a conscious effort to try and keep myself out of hospital emergency rooms.

One of the more mysterious incidents which occurred involving Christina happened when we were over two hundred miles from home. I had just crept her over a speed bump at about one mile an hour when I suddenly found her to be permanently "out-of-gear". We were in neutral in all four gears. Five, including reverse.

Turned out the rear axle had snapped. Christina was towed the two hundred-plus miles home for repair.

My personal favorite, somewhat "Hitchcock-ian Type" incident occurred on the downward side of a steep mountain when the metal pin connecting Christina's accelerator pedal to her set of dual carburetors unexpectedly came loose.

After a couple miles of hurtling down the treacherous mountain roads at full throttle, I was finally able to descend to an area of fairly level grade, and managed to downshift Christina to a stop.

The day I put her up for sale, her clutch went out. I mean ALL THE WAY OUT. In her final act of defiance, when confronted with being sold, Christina threw a tantrum and refused to budge.

With most cars, replacing the clutch means replacing the clutch. Mechanically, with Christina, removing the clutch meant first having to REMOVE THE ENGINE! My dad and I bought a how-to book, rented some equipment, hoisted the engine out and got it done.

I sold Christina to the first person who answered the ad. He was a young guy, like me. I told him everything that was wrong with the car and he bought it, anyway.

A week later, he was back on my doorstep, begging me to take the car back. I felt bad for him, but I just couldn't do it.

I should've done the world a favor before I sold it. I should have driven the car back to those mountains, found the highest cliff, and let 'er go. But not before I put a quarter on the front seat so I could legally say that I lost something.

PART 10
HOLIDAZE

FORTY-TWO
A VERY BRADY CHRISTMAS

T'was (nearly) the night before Christmas, and all through the house, not a creature was stirring, not even a mouse. That was the problem. I was willing to give anyone, even a pharmaceutical rodent, a fifty-dollar bill if they could just present me with a single bottle of that stomach-soothing, pinked, medicinal chaser known as Pepto-Bismol.

It was one o'clock in the morning and I was sprawled upon the hotel bed in digestive distress. My misery illuminated by the wanton flickering's of a color TV.

The hotel store had closed hours ago. The same hotel store which, when open, offered guests shot-glass-sized portions of Pepto for ten bucks. A bargain at any price, particularly at one A.M.

My four frequent traveling companions and myself were sharing the room. They were all scattered about in careless, inconsiderate states of slumber. There was micro—cattle baron Rural Randy, and his lovely, yet equally unconscious wife, Mary.

In the far corner, snoozed Mango Mick, named not only for his affinity for the delectable tropical fruit, but also for his frequent implication of the fruit as the singular source for a series of mysterious, recurring rashes.

The final member of our predominantly unconscious group was

Seaplane Cindy, so christened after an ill-fated aviational island hop during which she unexpectedly exhibited an inclination toward air sickness by reexperiencing her lunch.

So, there I was, lying in a strange bed, in a strange room, in Key West.

In fact, just when I thought things couldn't get any stranger, a very strange television program, with a very strange, yet very seasonal title of "A Very Brady Christmas" appeared upon the TV screen.

For the most part, "A Very Brady Christmas" featured nearly all of the original actors and actresses who had appeared in the original 1970's sitcom "The Brady Bunch" of which I used to be an occasional viewer in my younger days.

The movie began as had the TV show, with "The Bunches" ensquared, grided heads, unabashedly grinning at us, and at each other.

While the basic theme of the TV series centered around the family conflicts which developed between persons when a woman with three girls marries a man with three boys, the movie also deals with that recurring Brady-ian theme of family conflicts when all the kids and their families reunite at Ma and Pa Brady's for Christmas.

As I watched the show, I found myself beginning to shout aloud at the TV, making occasional remarks about the direction of the dialogue, the predictability of the plot, and the sappiness of vividly staged, hokey, melodic outbursts of the Brady's into Christmas song.

My remarks succeeded not only in making me feel better, but also in awakening my fellow traveling companions. After verbally assailing me for my noise, and unable to immediately return to sleep, they joined me in watching the televised melee until the end.

Somewhere in between, a disoriented Mango Mick arose and attempted to relieve himself in the closet, while Seaplane Cindy suddenly burst into an unseasonal, unsolicited, medley of musical selections previously attributed to The Village People.

At the end of "A Very Brady Christmas", Brady patriarch Mike, is called to the only construction site in America where construction workers actually work on Christmas Day. A job where two security guards have become trapped just inside the entrance of a collapsed building.

As the project's former architect, Brady is required to dash into the collapsed structure and rescue the two men while all of the other workers, police, paramedics, the entire Brady family, the media, and a multitude of spectators who apparently have nothing better to do on Christmas Day, stand by and watch.

Brady goes in. The two previously trapped men stagger out while Brady becomes trapped inside, in a seemingly uncomfortable standing position by a fallen cardboard beam.

At this moment, the assembled Brady clan suddenly burst into song. Amongst the melodic warbling of "Come All Ye Faithful", Mike Brady suddenly emerges from the structure with only a slightly dusty jacket as evidence of his ordeal.

Understandably, at movie's end, I found that I wasn't the only person in that hotel room who could have benefited from the contents of a bottle of the pink stuff.

FORTY-THREE
STUFFED TURKEYS

Stand up! Look at your toes! Or, as in my case, try to - no matter the abdominal contour. Join me in the rallying cry of the turkey: "Gobble!" (pause here for dramatic effect) "Gobble! Gobble! Gobble!"

Gobble? I know I did! Is there not something ironic in the cry of the turkey?

What did we have for Thanksgiving? Turkey! What did we have for Christmas? Turkey! What did we have for New Year's? Turkey — turkey stuffed with black-eyed peas for good luck, and a ham on the side.

Turkey. Turkey. Turkey. Ham.

Gobble. Gobble. Gobble. Oink! Hmmmm, maybe there's a correlation there.

T'was "the time to be jolly". How can one be jolly without a forkful of gigged turkey in one hand, and a pint full of holiday cheer in the other? I was merely fulfilling our traditional interpretation of the holiday season.

By ancestorial precedent, i.e. pilgrims and such, holidays cannot be officially celebrated unless all participants attack tablefuls of overly abundant food, with a flurry of overly polished forks, and a clash of cutlery. It was all quite innocent, legal, and yet, quite fulfilling - apparently overly so.

But what can be expected of a season which is spirited and championed by an overweight man attired in a bright red suit?

Oh, we were warned, as we were every year. The "Red Rotund One" always appears at the end of the nationally televised Macy's Thanksgiving Day Parade to model our upcoming "holiday physique". It is a physique profoundly developed and shaped by "cuisinial intake" (i.e. "eating") by persons whose catch phrase "It's not the heat, It's the humidity, is seasonally replaced with "I ate too much. I must have gained ten pounds", while contentedly, yet proudly, thumping their bellies as they would that of the hull of a home-grown, prize-winning melon.

Of course, there were holiday meals of the aforementioned turkey and ham, with dizzying side dishes of various salads, stuffing (a.k.a. "dressing"), green beans, peas, mashed potatoes, sweet potatoes, cranberries, large slabs of hot cornbread salved with hot butter, steaming hot biscuits, squash casseroles smothered in cheese sauce, candies, cookies, cakes, flakey crusted pies of apple, and of pumpkin, etc., etc. (note: "etc." is the only pre-coma-ed item in this sentence which does not contain any calories).

I enthusiastically did my part to partake in the offerings. It was, in fact, while I was cramming myself with cranberries in a celebration of Thanksgiving that Grandma Gladiolus began yammering forth a dissertation of her very latest in an ongoing series of delightful "Inpatient" medical adventures and procedures in graphic, stomach—churning detail.

Grandma G. celebrated each of the three-day holiday meals with said dissertation, which only seemed to grow in length and in detail with each unsummoned, repeat performance.

If there had been just one more national or international holiday booked on her "Gallstone Tour", I feel certain that I would have had to politely excuse myself from the table and then climbed to the top of the roof of the house in King Kong fashion, and swan dived to the awaiting turf below.

Entertainment aside, like many successful meals (much like successful TV series'), there were "spinoff meals" (until the leftovers weren't left). Meals like turkey omelets, turkey toast, turkey—flavored oatmeal, peanut butter and turkey sandwiches, the original turkey sandwich, the original turkey sandwich "au gratin", turkey casseroles, Turkeys Rockefeller, blackened Turkey (sometimes created by accident), jello-ed turkey, fillet of turkey, turkey pot pies, turkey pies, Turkeys Jubilee, and many others, restricted only by the boundaries of the frazzled, frantic, "turkeyed-out", post-holiday mind.

And so, the holidays are gone for another year. And we are again left with the "Ghost of Multiple Forkfuls Past".

The problem, is that the ghost is not an invisible one - quite the contrary. The Ghost of Multiple Forkfuls Past has become the "Baggage of Body—Present".

Due to the holiday season (a.k.a. "The season of "F-O-O-D", I am entering this year as I entered the last: with "Body Au Beachball". But that is what New Year's resolutions are for. That is also what Christmas gifts such as spleen-colored sweatsuits, gift memberships to gyms and fitness clubs, and also what grit-filled milkshakes, and ADJUSTABLE bathroom scales are for.

As for myself, of late I've been pressing the accelerator a bit closer to the floor whenever I'm driving by any ongoing livestock auctions.

Gobble! Gobble!

FORTY-FOUR
SEASON TO TASTE

This holiday season, let us take a few moments to review the historical role of the adult male in the preparatory process of the holiday meal.

Whereas he was once THE family "Breadwinner", he is now very often "Co—Breadwinner", at best. He can also be categorized as "Bread-slicer", as his historical role in the preparation of holiday meals remains primarily restricted to the slicing and delving out of "over-glorified chicken parts"; a.k.a. turkey drumsticks, turkey wings, turkey gizzards, and such.

For over a hundred years or so he has been performing the same conciliatory holiday task and has received little or no opportunity for advancement, or promotion. This is, of course, blatant sexual discrimination.

Many women in this country are of the opinion that the adult American male becomes helpless if he encounters an item in the food chain which does not have a pop-top, or the international symbol for "Tear Here".

Nothing could be farther from the truth. This is because contrary to popular feminine opinion, a lot of us men know how to cook. To a degree.

For the most part, males begin cooking when they leave their parent's house and get out on their own. Unfortunately, the adolescent male's initial definition of "cooking" may have little or nothing to do with the inside of a kitchen.

But eventually, he is forced into the helm of an actual kitchen, driven by elements he does not fully understand - such as the actual contents of the college cafeteria's "Special of the day".

I know this, because like many men, I commenced and honed my cooking skills in the collegiate culinary plain. What I initially lacked in culinary abilities, and in presentation, I tried to make up for in creativity.

Of course, this resulted in threats upon my life by unimaginative, unappreciative, knife and fork-wielding roommates.

My first original dish, and my culinary debut, was a creation I called "Asian-Cowboy Food". The primary ingredients of the recipe were rice and beans. In fact, they were not only the primary ingredients, they were the only ingredients.

My fascination with potential variations of Western cuisine continued when I created my next dish, which I appropriately dubbed "Cow Pie Stew".

I actually discovered the dish quite by accident when I failed to promptly clean out a saucepan which contained three-day-old remnants of Asian-Cowboy Food.

Becoming bored with semi-domestic creations, I decided to "go abroad" for my next culinary excursion. I decided to go Italian and bought a frozen pizza. It seemed a promising culinary choice. It had directions. I could read.

I took the pizza out of its wrapper and preheated the conventional oven to 350 degrees. I say "conventional oven" because back then the only "microwave" that I was aware of was a rare form of greeting between two passing, amiable amoebas on a dampened microscope slide.

I slid the still-frozen pizza onto the middle rack of the heated vehicle and closed the door.

The pizza manufacturer's instructions stated that the pepperoni-ed product would be ready in 15 minutes.

It was not.

While the cheese topping appeared to be properly melted, and the pepperoni prudently curled, the pizza's underbelly stubbornly remained pale and uncooked.

Another 15 minutes and the top of the pizza had become a charred, unforgiving, culinary wasteland. The only concession that the underside of the pizza had made was a set of perfectly paralleled, blackened grill marks.

A moment later, the cleverly disguised, cardboard pizza bottom burst into flames.

In retrospect, if the majority of us cuisine-ially inept men were to arise and attempt a culinary coup, taking over the holiday meal cooking from our officially designated culinary kahuna's, the results would most probably be culinarily-catastrophic, leading to flashback semblances of Asian-Cowboy Food, Cow Pie Stew, and Napalmed Pizzas. This option versus our historic culinary holiday role of delving out tasty, over-glorified chicken parts.

Hmmm ...

On behalf of my culinary-oppressed brethren everywhere, I have but one thing to say: Can I get you a wing or a drumstick?

PART 11
LOOKING BACK

FORTY-FIVE

BACK TO THE BAIT WELL (1996)

Looking back from this distance, it is hard for me to tell exactly when my childhood came to an end. It may have been when I stopped watching Saturday morning cartoons on TV. Or when I lost interest in gluing together plastic model airplanes. Or maybe when I stopped reading Mad Magazine.

In actuality, it was probably 1963 in Prattville, Alabama, when for the first time, I experimentally killed a fellow inhabitant of this earth with a destructive "pop" of my new Daisy BB rifle.

I will never forget the sickening sensation that came over me as I watched the irreversible death plummet of that sparrow. And with it, my childhood.

In the days and years to follow, I got older. Somewhat wiser, but certainly older. I learned a lot of things in Prattville, Alabama. I learned about responsibilities, and about growing up. I learned how to mow the lawn, and how to take out the garbage.

I also learned about the fragility of life.

By most accounts, I have since grown up. I do not shoot animals anymore, although I do still mow the lawn and take out the garbage on a regular basis.

And now, I would give anything to be able to reach back and touch my childhood once again.

That is why recently, I had to go back to The Bait Well.

I have lived some of the most wonderful days of my life behind that little gray clapboard house on the southeast corner of Glendale and Troy in Lakeland, Florida.

Back then, the rambling metal roof above the outdoor minnow-filled concrete block tanks lent shade to a pair of out-of-breath boys, pedaling their bicycles, chasing a hot summer sun.

The Bait Well's owners, O. B. Hannah and his wife Tressie were kind, gentle, easy-going folks who welcomed all-comers, even curious, cash-poor little boys trying to beat the summer heat.

My Bait Well days were consumed with riding bicycles with tall handlebars and banana seats. Of short pants and Buster Brown shoes.

Of kneeling bare-kneed in the dirt and dust, in order to shoot marbles called "perrys" and "cats-eyes " from the deadly aim of a thumb and forefinger.

Of twisting apart the halves of Oreo cookies in order to scrape the sweet, dried white cream out with a bottom row of eagerly accommodating teeth.

Of laying back on the cool, lush green blades of a lawn in order to lazily observe the shapes and sizes of the white puffy clouds as they drifted across a brilliantly blue Southern sky.

Dropping a dime allowed you to pull a bottled cold drink from the rack along the side of the red Coca-Cola machine, positioned along the outside wall of The Bait Well's little store.

Noisily bubbling air pumps in the concrete block fish tanks invited the attention and the curiosity of even the thirstiest of little boys.

I will never forget the orchestral chirping of the hundreds of bait crickets from inside The Bait Well's little store. Everything from worms, to nightcrawlers, to fishing hooks, to fishing lures, to bobbers, to candy bars,to cane poles, to those crickets, were offered for sale in that little store.

I can remember the long-billed khaki fishing hat that Mr. Hannah used to wear. And his wire-rimmed glasses.

I remember the kindness of his smile, and of his ways, and how he always took the time to talk to everyone; even to a little boy who loved fishing almost as much as he loved The Bait Well.

Although Mr. Hannah died back in the summer of 1976, his wife Tressie continued carrying on The Bait Well tradition he had started, for another 19 years by herself.

Last summer, Mrs. Hannah suffered two back-to-back heart attacks. She is at home now, resting and recovering comfortably, but she had to close The Bait Well in June of last year, after her first heart attack, although she continues to sell boxes of worms to devout customers from the porch of her house.

At age 88, Tressie Hannah attributes her remarkable recovery to God, family, and friends. In that order.

When I paid her a recent visit, Mrs. Hannah was indulging her life-long passion for basketball by watching an Orlando Magic basketball game on TV.

For a short while Mrs. Hannah reminisced about the bygone days of The Bait Well. Her face lit up whenever she spoke about her late husband O.B.

It seems nothing lasts forever. Not the visit. Not even the Bait Well.

Before I left, Tressie Hannah wanted to be sure that I included a message of thanks in her behalf to all of the hundreds of Polk County fishermen who had visited The Bait Well during its 44 years.

But most of all, thank *you*, Mrs. Hannah. Thank *you*.

FORTY-SIX
PURSUIT TO PRATTVILLE (1997)

I drank a toast to Jimmy Herman the other day.

Appropriately, it was with a bottle of RC Cola. When we were kids, Jimmy and I used to drink a lot of RC Cola together. That was back in 1963, when we were both eight years old, growing up in and around the woods of Prattville, Alabama.

Back then, Jimmy had convinced me that you could actually drink an RC Cola in a returnable glass bottle if you sucked hard enough on the little round dent at the bottle's bottom edge.

I know that RC's stock had to have jumped up at least a couple of points during the many weeks that I purchased a couple hundred of apparently defective, glass returnable bottles of RC Cola, while attempting to defy the laws of both physics, and common sense.

The bottle of RC Cola with which I toasted Jimmy was plastic. Plastic was the only kind of RC bottle that I could find. Times change. So did Prattville, Alabama. We left in 1964. My brother was six. I was nine. We had both enjoyed the best year of our childhood there.

Back then we shucked and ate pecans from the large, plentiful pecan tree behind our carport. When we weren't eating them, we were throwing them. Usually at each other.

Our backyard descended into a long, narrow, abandoned railroad track bed which wound through the town like a red clay snake. The railroad tracks behind our house had long since been removed, before we'd even lived there.

Just across the red clay railroad bed, were the woods. Not just any woods. *Our* woods. Although we never did know who legally owned them. Truth is, we never really thought about it, and it never came up.

Along with Jimmy, and the Jones boys next door, we spent many hours in those woods, running, playing, building forts, and squirting each other with water pistols filled with water from the wood's trickling spring. All while a palomino horse we'd appropriately named "Trigger" grazed in a pasture nearby.

That was 1964. It had been 33 years since my brother, and I had walked upon the streets of Prattville. Pursuing a sudden recent whim, we returned.

Prattville had changed a lot, as towns are apt to do in 33 years. There were a lot of additions, like the Interstate, a lot of fast-food restaurants, and a few additional stores.

We arrived in late afternoon and ate supper at a fast-food chain store "Chicken house" that had been built on the corner of our old residential street. When we'd finished, we took a leisurely walk down the old street for the first time in over three decades.

We recognized the small, red brick house immediately when we saw it. Sadly, the old pecan tree was gone. The railroad bed had been sodded over, and was now, backyard. Trigger and his pasture were long gone. Worst of all, the central portion of what had once been our wonderful woods was now a steak house parking lot.

Yet, with all those changes, we still managed to find Jimmy Herman's mom. Although her husband had passed away a few years back, and the kids had all grown, moved away, and started families of their own, she'd never left the home she'd known since 1954. The home that was next to the one we'd lived in all those years ago.

She was sweet and spry and wonderful, at 79. She filled us in on who was doing what, what had happened to whom, and graciously enhanced our education with family photos and a round of cold drinks.

By Mrs. Herman's direction, we managed to find the old red brick elementary school where I had attended 3rd grade. While my brother and I stood studying the school from the parking lot, a young man of about 30, toting a five-gallon bucket, approached us, asking if he could be of assistance.

When I told him that I'd attended the school when I was a little boy, he stuck out his hand and proudly told us he had just been appointed the school's new principal. He was there along with a maintenance crew, getting the summer-vacant building ready for the fall term.

He led us inside the building, where I walked upon oak plank floors which I had not strode upon since I was nine years of age.

Telling the gracious, enthusiastic, new principal that I had been eight years old, and in that building on November 22, 1963, when President Kennedy had been assassinated, put the time span into perspective for him. And, for me.

He expressed his measure of the three decades plus, time span with a single word: "Wild!" he exclaimed, shaking his head. We thanked him for his generosity and wished him the very best of luck in his new position.

We also visited Kiddie College, my brother's old kindergarten school of which he retained pleasant, vivid memories. Amazingly, Mrs. Creamer, his kindergarten teacher 33 years ago, was still there. She's now the school's Director, running the facility, along with Executive Director Mrs. Owens, who'd been the school's Director when my brother had attended kindergarten there.

While Mrs. Creamer graciously took my brother and myself on an extensive tour of the classrooms and playgrounds of Kiddie College, I unwittingly took extensive videos of the walls and floors and ceilings of the facility.

Fortunately, I also managed to also take some footage of Mrs. Creamer, Mrs. Owens, and my brother.

All of the people we met, and all of the people we visited were wonderful. Much like the year of our childhood had been in Prattville. My brother and I both agreed that we'd like to have been able to have spent much more of our childhood there.

Neither of us could accept the fact that those 33 years had passed so quickly.

Wild. Just wild.

FORTY-SEVEN
CROSSING BACK TO CROSSLAND
(1998)

It began as it had ended. With a song. James Taylor's rendition of "You've Got a Friend". We'd selected it as our official class song before we'd graduated Crossland High School in 1973.

That was a few years ago. My thoughts drifted back all of those years, and back to the song because I'd received some erroneous mail announcing a high school class reunion scheduled for late August 1998. Erroneous because the document declared the event to be a 25-year reunion.

Surely it could not have been 25 years since I'd last driven Dad's white 1966 Mustang over the speed bumps leading into the high school parking lot. Surely it could not have been 25 years since I last walked the locker-lined, hallowed halls of my old high school; since I'd run my last track meet; since I'd said goodbye to adolescence, high school friends and embarked upon life. But, it was.

Regardless, I'd already decided that I would not be attending the reunion. Then I saw the album.

Since its release, I'd always wanted to own a copy of James Taylor's 1993 double CD "Live" but had been deterred by its somewhat lofty full retail price.

A few years after the CD's release, I'd seen a used, discounted copy in a music store, hesitated, then returned to buy it, only to find that it was gone. I told myself that if I ever found it discounted in a used CD rack again, I'd snatch it up.

I looked for years. Then, a month before the 25th high school reunion, I found it. I flashed back to the first James Taylor album I'd ever purchased. The year was 1971. The album was a banana-yellow-colored 8-track tape entitled "Mud Slide Slim and the Blue Horizon".

I triumphantly took Taylor's 1993 Live CD home, sat down, and listened to the entire album while gazing outward through my living room window, into a sub-tropical backyard that was a thousand miles, and 25 years from high school.

For the most part, the tunes were warm and familiar, although I felt a dampness enter my eyes when I heard Taylor sing the opening strains to "Fire and Rain". Like Taylor, I'd lost a friend also.

Ironically, I'd met her at our 10-year high school reunion back in 1983. She was tragically killed in a car crash in 1986.

By the time "You've Got a Friend" came on at the album's end, I knew I had to go back. For her. For me. It was time to take stock of my 43-year-old, un-CEO-esque, never-married, childless life.

The day after my 43rd birthday I boarded a plane at Tampa International Airport in order to fly back into time.

Two hours later, at Ronald Reagan Washington National Airport in Washington D.C., I was greeted by the gracious boyhood friend with whom I'd be staying.

As we climbed up the back steps of his sturdy, red brick suburban Maryland home, we stepped past a large jar of sun tea which was brewing on the back porch.

After receiving warm, affectionate greetings from my friend's wife and their 12-year-old daughter, I brought up the pleasantly familiar subject of the sun tea, to which his wife informed me that it was getting late in the year for brewing sun tea. The late summer sun was waning. That particular jar might be the last that they would be able to brew until the following year.

My friend and I sat down at the kitchen table and recounted old times for a couple of hours. Then, it was time to get ready to go to the reunion dance.

That evening, the facility at which our event was being held was hosting two different high school reunions. When we walked into the room in which ours was supposedly being held, I thought I'd walked into the wrong room. All of the people in the room I'd entered were middle-aged.

While most of the women looked great, it was the state of the men's hair which immediately affected me. Some of their hair was white, some gray, some gone. Where were my 18-year-old classmates? What had "they" done with them?

Then here and there I'd see a glimmer of familiarity in a middle-aged face. She kind of looks like ... He looks a little like ... Add 25 years and ... wow, it was them! And it was me.

I had not seen many of them for the 15 years which had passed since I'd attended the 10-year reunion. Some I hadn't seen for 25. Where had the years gone? How could they have gone so fast? We had thought we were going to be young forever! Some of my old classmates had kids at home who were as old as we were when we graduated high school – when we'd started this gig.

Despite the years, and the tens of thousands of meals we'd consumed since graduation, kids, hefty mortgages, and slowing metabolisms, all in all, we still looked great.

In fact, a lot of the women "still had it". Many looked as attractive that evening as they had in high school. Some even looked more so.

As for the guys, we were holding our own. At one point during the evening, the friend with whom I was staying and another high school buddy of ours we'd found, were standing near the bar as guys are apt to do, when our mutual friend remarked that we were the three "youngest looking guys in the room". A generous compliment for which we probably should have paid him cash.

The next day we had beautiful weather for our reunion picnic. The picnic was relaxing. There were kids and lots of food. While a few classmates made it to the picnic who hadn't made it to the dinner dance, there were a few whom I'd seen the night before and hadn't had a chance to say "hi" to who didn't make it to the picnic.

Many of us continued conversations began the evening before. And started new ones. It was great just being together again. Even after 25 years, the bond was still there. Familiar faces searching for familiar faces. Hearing names and seeing faces which we had not heard or seen for so many years. We basked in it all.

Then, it was time to go. Time to return to the real world and to our real lives, once again.

On the flight home, amid all of my 25-year high school reunion memories, I could not help but reflect back on my own life, and back to that late-summer jar of sun tea on my friend's back porch.

Guess it was a little later in the season than I'd thought.

FORTY-EIGHT
THE CASA, BEAR, AND ME – (CIRCA 1990)

It is where I go once a year to get away. It is a town rich with a history of a calamitous nature. Painted with broad, bold, brushstrokes of color. A town once of buccaneers, of merrily drunken sots who purposely lured ships up onto their reef and to their death, who then preyed upon the wrecked plunder as buzzards upon a freshly broken carcass. It is what they did - how they ate, how they drank, how they lived, how they survived. A ship's death gave them meat, and more importantly, drink, for the table.

Few places can claim the history and the notoriety of Key West. None, save her can claim the distinction of being 89 miles north of Cuba and of being the southernmost city in the United States.

The island's colorful past, present, and uniqueness has been the subject of many a book, movie, and song. All romanticized versions of Key West aside, it is an island which long ago lost its once boat-only-access isolation which once enabled island residents to exercise "particular liberties in a murky sea of legalities".

Key West's unique remoteness, the greatest contributing factor to its character and identity, began to fade with the thundering entrance of Standard Oil magnate Henry Flagler's "Overseas Railway", completed on January 22, 1912.

Although the Railway which linked the Keys to the mainland was destroyed by a hurricane in 1935, the bold, mangled venture was replaced with an "Overseas Highway".

The tiny 2 mile by 4-mile island at the end of US-1 was at one time residence for such authors as Ernest Hemingway and Tennessee Williams; of recording artist Jimmy Buffett and Captain Tony Tarracino.

It is a place where sunset beckons tourists from their motel and hotel rooms, restaurants, bars, shops, and beaches to the water's edge at Mallory Square. There, at that hour, the crowd gathers and the shows begin. Key West's talented and eccentric resident characters perform, illuminated by the glow of sunset - performing their acts for the entertainment and for the alms of intrigued tourists.

The performances vary as widely as do the individuals themselves. And individuals vary *very, very* widely in Key West. If not simply by their appearance, each performer is an act unto themselves. The acts run simultaneously, competing for audiences often with upturned, beckoning hats on the ground before them. The performers' talents vary as widely as do the individuals.

On any given day, the acts might include tightrope walkers, fire eaters, sword swallowers, magic, guitar—strumming singers, and then some.

One can walk from Mallory Square, along residential Whitehead Street, pass Ernest Hemingway's House, and at the end of the street, stop and gaze out over the ocean, and vainly strain to see the distant, invisible profile of the beleaguered island of Cuba from the Southernmost Point in the United States.

If one then walks left for a bit, and then takes a couple turns to the right, one comes upon 1500 Reynolds Street and the elegance of a hotel from an era past: The Casa Marina.

The Casa Marina (Spanish for "House by The Sea") was a dream of Henry Flagler, which he never lived to see fulfilled.

Sixteen months after completing his railway to Key West, Henry Flagler died in West Palm Beach on May 20, 1913, at age 83. In 1918, Flagler's company purchased six and a half acres of oceanfront property in Key West for $1,000 and shortly afterward, construction began on Flagler's Casa Marina Hotel.

Once completed, The Casa Marina had her Grand Opening on January 1, 1920. Key West now had a large, architecturally beautiful presence which introduced luxury on a grand scale to Key West's well-to-do tourists. In her early days, "The Casa" was a social magnet for America's big-name entertainers and her social elite, many enroute to Cuba.

Due to the superior engineering and meticulous construction of the structure, The Casa Marina survived the fury of the hurricane of 1935 with little damage.

During World War II, the Navy bought The Casa Marina and utilized the hotel as officer's quarters. In 1946, civilians purchased the hotel back from the government. During the Cuban Missile crisis in 1962, the Army took up its headquarters in the hotel. After the crisis, a plan by the Army to make the hotel a permanent headquarters failed.

Efforts to convert The Casa Marina into a retirement home were interrupted by the purchase of the hotel by a local Senator. For a decade, the hotel was vacant. The Senator died in 1975, and The Marriott Corporation purchased the Hotel in 1978. They spent a year and a half and over thirteen million dollars to modernize The Casa and to restore it to its former splendor, reopening on May 24, 1979. The hotel has since gone through three owners (as of around 1990).

Today, The Casa Marina is a gorgeous, living monument to Florida's past. The Casa has 312 rooms which are tastefully decorated with elegant simplicity, reflecting the era in which the hotel was constructed.

Its exterior walls are creamy of color, accented by an orange tiled roof, gleaming in the island's brilliant, tropical sun. Like her sister Flagler hotels in St. Augustine, Palm Beach, and Miami, The Casa Marina is principally Spanish in architecture.

The centerpiece of the circle driveway out front which greets the guests is a hand painted, brilliantly colored wall mural which features a portrait of Henry Flagler, a tropical sun glistening off of the ocean, and a scene of what the viewer might have seen in that very spot had he been standing there several decades earlier.

Upon entering the cool, dim, lobby, one is stepping back into a

Florida grandeur of time gone by. The floors are of darkened hardwood, the high interior walls, a cool, creamy white. Dark wooden beams traverse the ceiling overhead. To the right, upon the entry wall, is a white mantel fireplace with a large throw rug of the period stretched at its hearth. Four white, wicker chairs and a glass-topped coffee table rest atop the ornate rug, awaiting the pleasure of their guests.

Back of the hotel is a covered walkway, bordered by a restaurant patio, complete with circular tables with sprouting umbrellas to shield dining guests from the hot, tropical sun. Farther, toward the ocean, is the pool - cool, clear, and refreshing, complimented by strategically placed healthy, green-topped palm trees whose long, green, fibrous fingers are gently sifted by a lazy breeze off the nearby ocean.

On the hotel's private, white sandy beach is the "Sun-Sun"- an open-air lounge where the parched of soul and the parched of throat can find refreshment.

It is where I sit once a year, gazing seaward. My only material accompaniments are a pair of swim trunks, a pair of flipflops, a room key, and a lean collection of short, expensive cigars. It is there where I push away current news and world affairs and begin to absorb the soothing sounds and sights of the gently breaking waves and the sparkling, becalming ocean while I contemplate such things as the horizon and the curvature of the earth.

After some time, when I can finally summon the energy, I collect up my remaining cigars and shuffle down the beach, toward the "Watersports Shack" and the boat dock, to see how my friend "Bear" is doing. Bear is not truly a bear but is a dog of sorts - a combination of breeds. He is an intense, yet simple personality, whose life revolves around his greatest love: fishing.

Bear is large and brown of fur and eyes. His home is down the street from The Casa Marina. While his owner is at work, Bear walks down the street, to the hotel's beach whenever he feels like it, which is often. If he is not lounging on the beach, or leisurely sprawled upon the floor, beneath the lazy, whirling ceiling fan of the open-aired Watersports Shack, he is fishing.

When the mood strikes him, Bear wades chest-deep out into the ocean and peers downward, into the glimmering water before him.

Head down, ears out, brow furrowed in concentration while his large, intense, eyes peer downward for unwitting crabs or fish.

The only hint that the observer has that Bear is enjoying himself is an occasional "Yip!"

and a scurried wag of that nub of a tail.

Fishing is serious business for Bear. He does not acknowledge any offered attempts at distraction, nor does he tolerate interruptions of any kind. Even while he is at rest, lounging on the beach, he treats any attention he receives with the greatest of indifference.

When he is through fishing and has had enough of the beach scene, Bear casually walks back down the street to his owner's house.

In the four years Bear has been a fleeting, special guest at The Casa Marina, no one can recall his catching any fish, or anything else, for that matter. But catching fish is not what is truly important to Bear. For Bear, what is truly important is to do what he enjoys best.

I miss Bear. I wish I was down there right now.

But then, I already am.

PART 12
BEST FRIENDS

FORTY-NINE
KEY WEST AND THE BEAR (1995)

Over the many years I've been making vacation visits to Key West, I've certainly met an array of colorful characters; the most memorable of whom happens to be a dog named Bear.

About five years ago, I was walking along the beach behind Marriott's Casa Marina Hotel in Key West when I first saw him. He was fishing. Fishing was what Bear loved to do more than anything else in the world.

He would wade out into the warm, tropical ocean of Key West, until he was about chest deep. Then, like the truly dedicated fisherman he was, Bear would wait.

Patiently. His ears pricked upward in anticipation. His forehead frowned in concentration, his brown eyes focused downward, peering intently into the clear, shimmering water below. Every short brown hair on his body was bristled and on high alert.

Bear would react to the sighting of even one of his audacious, finned quarry with a series of deep, joyous barks, as a shudder of excitement raced through his large, muscular frame, jarring his mere stub of a tail into an enthusiastic, wagging frenzy.

Bear considered fishing to be a serious business. He did not acknowledge any offered attempts at distraction by intrigued human spectators, like myself. Nor did he tolerate interruptions of any kind. Even while at rest, lounging in the sparse shade along the beach, Bear treated any unsolicited human attention which he received with the greatest of indifference.

When I recently arrived at the Casa Marina in Key West after a two-year absence, I immediately realized that something was terribly wrong. It was early morning, and Bear was not out there, fishing. He was nowhere to be seen.

As I uneasily walked down to the Casa Marina's Watersports building to inquire as to Bear's whereabouts, I tried to be optimistic. Maybe Bear and his owner had moved away.

"Bear died a couple of years ago, " the young man behind the counter told me.

I felt my throat tighten and my heart sink.

"He died before I started working here, but I 've heard a lot about him, " the young man continued. "He's a legend around here. In fact, we 've even got his picture on the wall," he said proudly, pointing to an eight by ten photograph of Bear on the wall behind him.

Ironically, I discovered that Bear's former owner now works in the sales department at the Casa Marina. Her name is Stacey Mitchell. She is 33 and is proud to emphasize that she was "Bear's Mom".

"I rescued him," she recalls. "I was living in a dorm in Tampa at the time, attending the University of South Florida. I went to a humane center in Tampa with a friend who had gone there on some business.

"I saw this large dog in this small cage, and I asked them to let him out. He ran into my arms and licked my face.

"Bear Dog was a Labrador Retriever–Boxer mix. He was nine months old. He'd been locked up in a twelve-by-twelve room at a gas station. He slept, ate, urinated, and defecated in that room, until someone reported the situation to the humane society, and they picked him up and took him to their facility. If the animals were unclaimed after 30 days, they put them down. Bear Dog was on day 28 when I saw him, " she remembers.

"When I got to that shelter, I had no intention of getting a dog. I was living in a college dorm. But I couldn't let him die. For thirty dollars, I got to save Bear Dog."

After Mitchell adopted Bear, she made some immediate sacrifices in his behalf.

Within two weeks, she had rented an off-campus apartment that allowed dogs, and had gotten a job in order to support her new responsibility, while still attending classes at USF.

In return for her commitment, she received Bear's unconditional love, exhibited every minute she sat in a campus classroom, while he faithfully waited outside the classroom door for her return.

Mitchell recalls that Bear's early interest in fishing began with a couple of 50-gallon aquariums which she kept in her bedroom. Just before she went to bed every night, Mitchell would turn on the aquarium lights and feed the fish, while Bear watched, lying on her bed. He would get extremely jealous of the attention she was giving the fish, and he would bark, often climbing on furniture, trying to get his paws into the aquarium.

"In 1984, two years after I rescued Bear Dog, we moved to Key West. Bear Dog thought that the ocean was a large aquarium," Mitchell explains with amusement. "I only saw him catch a fish once. He quickly ate it whole, promptly threw it up, and went right back to fishing. It got to where everybody in Key West knew him."

Bear had a specific schedule to his day. He would leave home at 8:20 every morning and would walk down the block to the Watersports building at the Casa Marina, arriving promptly at 8:30. After greeting all of his human friends, he would fish for hours.

One month, the Watersports crew named Bear "Watersports Employee of the Month" for his perfect attendance record. They took his picture, and posted it up on the wall where it still is today. (1995)

After Bear left the Casa, he'd walk along the nearby county beach, and then walk the mile or so to Smathers Beach to check things out there.

During the hottest part of the day, Bear would return to the Casa and sleep on the beach in the shade beneath the rental Hobie Cat Sailboats.

"He'd always wake up in time to arrive at Louie's Backyard (a nearby outdoor bar) for happy hour, " Mitchell recalls. "He'd sit and wait for the bartender at Louie 's to bring him water from the cooler in a crystal glass drinking bowl they kept especially for him. If the water wasn't from the cooler; he wouldn't drink it."

Although Bear's fishing and social exploits would often require him to walk five miles or more a day, every night at six he'd be home on Mitchell's doorstep.

Being Bear's Mom has made Mitchell somewhat of a local celebrity in Key West.

When bartenders who knew Bear discovered her identity, they have bought both her husband David and herself rounds of drinks and entire meals.

"He was an icon, " Mitchell states simply.

The end came suddenly, and unexpectedly. Mitchell recognized that Bear was ill and rushed him to the veterinarian. He was quickly diagnosed with an advanced case of prostate cancer. He was in great pain and had only a few days in which to live. He was 13 years old.

Bear's last day was a Sunday, two years ago. Together, Mitchell and Bear walked down to Watersports at the Casa Marina, one last time.

"He could barely walk," Mitchell recalls sadly. He climbed up on a rock and looked down into the water. Then, he went and laid down while all his friends gathered around him and said 'goodbye'".

Mitchell was devastated.

"I had him cremated. His remains are now sitting atop a bookshelf in our home. For two years, my husband and I have talked about spreading his ashes over the ocean."

Today, Mitchell and her husband own a pair of young Weimaraner's and they believe that one of them just might be expressing an interest in going fishing.

They know just the place ...

FIFTY

SUGAR (1998)

One of the most touching newspaper cartoons I've ever seen appeared shortly after the untimely death of the late, great, syndicated newspaper columnist and humorist, Lewis Grizzard in 1994.

Drawn by co-worker Mike Luckovich of The Atlanta Constitution, the cartoon depicts Grizzard, typewriter in hand, as he approaches the Pearly Gates of heaven. Catfish, his beloved black Labrador Retriever who preceded him in passing, is happily trotting out the gates of heaven to meet him, tongue panting, and tail a-wag.

It is comforting to believe that when our own time comes, we will all be so lucky. Not only to make it to the Pearly Gates, but also to be greeted by one or more of our passed, beloved pets.

Me, I want to see Sugar again.

My folks paid a nominal adoption fee and rescued Sugar from our local county animal control facility. If she had not been adopted that day, she was scheduled to lose her life the next. She was quiet and meek and frightened.

The facility employees told Mom and Dad that she was about six months old and was already housebroken. Her previous owner had named her "Sugar" because in contrast to her long red coat, her dainty little paws were white, as if she'd stepped in sugar somewhere along her way.

Sugar had the coat and the shape of an Irish Setter, only on a much smaller, more graceful scale. Her face was similar to that of a Cocker Spaniel, although not precisely so. Her black, perfect little nose punctuated the end of a soft, red, miniature Setter-like muzzle. Her eyes were dark, gentle, and expressive. She stood about two feet tall and weighed around 40 pounds.

After taking her home, Sugar seemed grateful, yet restless in her new surroundings. She initially spent a great deal of time hiding behind the bed in Mom and Dad's bedroom.

Gradually, as the weeks passed, she became more familiar with her new surroundings and with her new family, spending less time in the bedroom and more time with us. Although throughout most of her life she would flee in terror whenever she'd see a broom or heard a sudden loud noise. Even a noise as mild as the rattling pages of a newspaper.

Once Sugar had settled into her new home, she made it clear that she did not like to be left alone. One of her early, favorite toys was a soft, plastic cheeseburger which squeaked whenever she squeezed it in her mouth. Although Sugar never really chewed on her toys very much, she frequently carried her cheeseburger about the house with her for company. She could often be found sprawled out beneath the dining room table, asleep, with her cheeseburger by her side.

Whenever Mom and Dad would return to the house after leaving Sugar home alone for a while, they would often find her cheeseburger carefully placed on the floor alongside their bed. The side of the bed on which she placed the cheeseburger varied. Sometimes it would be found on Dad's side. Sometimes she would walk all the way around the bed and gently place it on the floor along Mom's side.

Mom and Dad always interpreted Sugar's meaningful cheeseburger message as the same: an offering of her most treasured possession, if they would just not leave her alone again.

As a rule, Sugar was not prone to jumping up on furniture. The exception was winter nights when she would lay out in the backyard for hours, enjoying the crisp, cool air. After which she would dash into the house, sprint for the living room couch, leap up, immediately sit down and look at us with an excited, silly, sheepish look on her face, her ears drawn back, her mouth a-grin with a feigned, puffing pant, anxiously seeking our approval for her blatant breach of doggie-furniture etiquette. After our vocal reassurances she would finally lie down, relax, and gradually fall asleep.

For the most part, Sugar was very well behaved. Mom often referred to her as being "perfect". Although there were occasions when despite Mom's somewhat stern calls of "Sugar", she would nonchalantly trot out of view, into the house's side yard, drawn by exciting, mysterious new scents.

I heard her bark maybe a dozen times. She was not a barker. She was a licker.

Her tongue was long, soft, pink, and narrow. When she was not expressing her love by licking us, she'd often lick herself, particularly her left leg. Especially after eating a particularly tasty bite of food. Sometimes when she was fast asleep, the tip of her soft, pink tongue protruded out from between her front teeth.

When she was in the house and became excited, she'd often dash down the house's long hallway. Her excited sprint sounding more like a gallop.

Sugar was always happy. Always full of love. She loved to follow her mom around the house. Even outside. She would lie next to her mom in the front yard while she was gardening for hours just to be near her.

In fact, Sugar often preferred the company of ladies. Whenever Mom held her monthly ladies bridge group at the house, Sugar always enjoyed associating with the ladies. She was always a lady herself, often properly crossing her legs when she was lying down.

Throughout her life, Sugar was always dainty and always feminine. So much so that Mom often called her "Little Girl ". She loved milk bones, and she loved car rides - especially leaning into the turns.

For 13 years, Sugar was a large, constant part of our lives. Of our family. Through the good times, and the bad. She was always there for us. Year after year. Certainly, she would never die. She would be with us forever.

In the last two or three years of her life, Sugar became deaf. Still sweet and wonderful, yet deaf. Her small, delicate muzzle whitened with age.

One evening, toward the end of last year, Sugar's restlessness in the middle of the night awakened Dad and he got up to find her. He found her sitting awkwardly on the dining room floor, grimacing, staring blankly off into space.

We began finding Sugar's beloved milk bones uneaten, lying around the house. While she still had her keen enthusiasm for acquiring them, she had seemingly lost her appetite for them. Something was wrong.

It was cancer. An operation. A brief recovery.

Further tests revealed that the cancer had spread to her lymph nodes and beyond. Her intestines were balled up. She had a stone in her bladder.

The morning after these grim revelations, I went by Mom and Dad's to see Sugar.

No one was home.

No one.

I decided to drive to a nearby vacant house which my brother had recently purchased. By chance, Mom and Dad were there. They were alone. Mom greeted me on the doorstep. After exchanging somewhat awkward, searching pleasantries, Mom told me that they had just "said goodbye" to Sugar at the veterinarians.

I nodded knowingly and gave her a hug as I felt my eyes fill with tears. For the most part, Dad just sat in their parked car by himself, silently staring straight ahead.

I walked around the house, into the backyard in order to be by myself for a few minutes. Suddenly, the sun did not seem quite as bright as it had a few minutes earlier.

Life did not seem as sweet.

I felt a lump rise in my throat as the tears began to trickle down my cheeks. It was the same lump that would catch in my throat whenever I would enter my folk's house for weeks thereafter, my eyes searching for a glimpse of her, my ears straining for the jingle of her collar. Then realizing once again that she really was gone, never to return.

We called her "The Shoog", "Shoogie", "Little Girl", and of course, "

Sugar". The truth is, she 'll never really leave us. Her life and her memory will be a part of our lives forever.

She was special. We were lucky and so was she. My folks took a chance and she was given 13 years of life which she never would have had, and we received thirteen years of love.

Sugar taught us many things. Perhaps the most important thing she taught us was that pedigrees are for people. The only "papers" which should be considered when getting a dog is whether to train them over the *National* or the *Sports* section of the newspaper.

The next time you're thinking about getting a dog, don't think about pet stores or pedigrees, or payment plans. Think about unconditional love and about saving a life.

To adopt a dog or a cat, call your local animal control office.

To love one, call your heart.

FIFTY-ONE
THE HOUND OF THE BASSETVILLES

If famous literary detective Sherlock Holmes were to examine the substantially sized paw prints trod by my wife and I's current canine companion, and to understandably deduce them to be the footprints of a gigantic hound, he would be mistaken. Almost as mistaken as I was in never wanting to own a dog for reasons of selfishness. I did not want to get a dog and to love it, only to experience the heartbreak and grief when the pet passed away at the end of his much shorter than human, lifespan.

Yet, three years ago, as a childless middle-aged couple, my wife-to-be and I had felt a bit of an emptiness in our lives. That something was missing. We rationalized that at our time of life, it was a bit too late for kids, but it wasn't too late to at least think about getting a dog. While I was still selfishly hesitant about getting one, I confessed that I had always liked Basset Hounds and she replied that her late brother had also liked the breed.

We instinctively went to a nearby pet shop and found a cute, brown and white, blue-eyed Basset puppy, made all the more adorable after pet shop employees dressed him in a miniature Santa suit and allowed him to run about the store. My fiancé wanted to purchase him immediately, but I hesitated, not yet willing to let go of my selfishness, which was also accompanied by a nagging inner doubt about whether purchasing a puppy from a pet store

would be doing the right thing. I made a deal with my fiancé. We'd think about it, and if the puppy was still at the store when we returned a few days later, we'd buy him. She readily agreed.

When we returned to the store on the designated day, I was relieved, yet somewhat saddened to learn that the puppy had been sold and was no longer there. My fiancé was greatly disappointed. It was then that we began to talk about rescuing a dog. Saving a life.

My folks had rescued the last two dogs which they had owned and the dogs had proven to be wonderfully devoted pets and companions. Later, I would learn from an administrator at the County Sheriff's Animal Control facility that rescued dogs have a devout love and affection for their rescuers, because they correctly sense that their rescuers, their new owners, their "pet parents", have saved their lives.

We began our rescue operation with daily visits to the County Sheriff's Animal Control website and to the local S.P.C.A. website, as well, searching exclusively, and somewhat guiltily, for Basset Hounds. It was difficult to scroll past all of those other sad, possibly soon-to-be-euthanized, canine faces, as we discriminately looked for Basset Hounds.

We were about to broaden our search to include all dogs when I found a male Basset's mug shot on the County Sheriffs website. It was a close, facial shot. His prominent, light-colored muzzle, tipped by a black, practical, hound nose took up most of the photo. His ears were back, his mouth drawn closed in a concerned pout, a circled rope, a noose, hung loosely about his neck. He looked disheveled and extremely sad. I had to see him.

The next day while my fiancé was at work, I drove to the County Sheriff's Animal Control facility. There, a courteous, uniformed employee took me back to the dog's holding pen. They guessed his age to be about two years old. The Basset quietly walked up to me, wagging his tail, pressing the tip of his nose through the enclosure's wire fence, while his beagle cellmate jumped up and down, barking incessantly.

The Basset's back was black, his legs and face a light, reddish brown. His eyes were large, brown, and expressive. His front paws were huge, his fur matted and sticky. His tail never stopped wagging as he looked searchingly at me. He seemed genuinely happy to see me. I grinned and talked to him briefly as I would have a child, asking him how he was doing. I felt we had to have him but needed my fiancé to see him and get her approval.

I signed some initial adoption papers, reserving the dog until my fiancé would be able to get by and see him a couple of days later. Once there, she took him for a short walk, fell in love with him, and paid the nominal adoption fee which mandatorily included his being neutered. After the procedure, we would have to wait a few days before we could pick him up and bring him home.

When we were finally able to do so, and had gotten him outside the front door of the Animal Control facility, he just started walking. He was going nowhere in particular, just away from there. His coat was dull, sticky, and smelled awful. I held my breath, gathered him up, and put him on a clean towel in the back of the car and we drove him to his new home. Later, we discovered a long, jagged scar along the inside of his right rear leg and a series of what we speculated might have been cigarette burns on his head.

About the time we could have safely bathed him according to the Animal Control vet's post neutering surgical instructions, Beauregard, as my fiancé so aptly named him, suddenly came down with a chronic case of kennel cough from which we were not certain he would recover.

After weeks of worry, antibiotics, and some nebulizer treatments at our local vet's office, I knew he'd be all right when I walked into the bathroom one day and found about ten feet of toilet paper unrolled onto the floor from its wall-mounted holder. Finally, after nearly two months after we'd rescued him, our neighborhood vet finally gave us the okay to wash the stinky, furry fellow.

Beauregard has been a large part of our family for over three years now. He is quite the character and aside from toilet paper, has exhibited an affinity for all things plastic, and also for the multitude of toys in his toy box. Particularly, the squeaky ones.

At Christmastime, he has had to endure wearing an ill-fitting canine Santa costume, and has subsequently donned Santa hats for our annual family Christmas card photos. Holiday tasks which he has tediously endured with obvious humiliation.

Beauregard has been a great gift to us. He has greatly enriched our lives, and we cannot imagine our lives without him.

Back in the days of the Old West, if you found yourself with a rope around your neck, it pretty much meant that you were at the end of your life. In Beauregard's case, it meant that, and then some. It meant the end of one life and the beginning of another.

FIFTY-TWO
OUR SWEET BOY

Once when my wife and I were out to dinner with an old friend and aging family members, our friend quietly remarked, "These are the golden times".

Many of us are lucky enough experience "golden times" in our lives. Sometimes they can come from unlikely sources – such as from the lives of rescued, four-legged adoptees for instance. My wife and I were blessed to have experienced thirteen years of golden times through the life, love, and the companionship, of Beauregard, our beloved Basset Hound.

We rescued him from our local county animal control facility. His back and both sides of his body were black, while the remainder of his coat was "hound red" – a light brown with a reddish hue which also touched his head, ears, chest, legs, and his large, thick paws. His eyes were large, brown, and expressive. They estimated him to be about two years old.

Beauregard had the handsome, noble face of a hound and a sweet disposition, despite his apparently being mistreated by his previous owner as evidenced by being found wandering the streets with a rope around his neck, with what appeared to be cigarette burn scars atop his head and a large, lightning bolt-shaped scar on the inside of his right rear leg.

For the first week that we had him, he did not bark. A few days later, we finallyheard the slow, measured, deep baritone bark that he would exhibit throughout his life with us.

He had more personality than some people I've known. He was what my grandpa would have referred to as "a character". When we took him out on walks, he would seek out people, often wanting to cross streets in order to approach two-legged, fellow pedestrians in order to say "hello". He genuinely loved people, and he also loved attention.

His newly found pedestrian friends would fawn over him, attracted by his inviting, low-to-the-ground, disarming appearance – his long ears dangling and his friendly, tail-wagging disposition. They often referred to him as handsome and sweet. He was truly both, and then-some. He was our sweet boy.

Sometimes on walks he could become "hound-stubborn" and would suddenly stop, lower his body closer to the ground and clench the earth or the pavement with all four of his chubby paws. If he hunkered down and you wanted to go left, and he wanted to go right, you were going right.

Despite his canine status and affiliation, Beauregard was a shy pooper. While on walks, he did not like pooping in public and always tried to step behind a bush or a tree in order to conduct his personal business in privacy.

He only bit me once and I deserved it. I was trying to get him off the bed and he wasn't having it, so I began to pull him toward me, dragging him across the bed. He warned me with a continual growl, but I continued to pull. Finally, he snapped and caught me on the bridge of my nose.

Unlike most Bassets, Beauregard was a picky eater. As a result, he never got fat and kept in pretty good shape, although he was partial to treats and to his doggie ice cream which he received on Wednesday and Saturday nights. If we asked him if his ice cream was "good" while he was licking it in its small plastic cup, his broad, lengthy tongue would pause for a moment while he considered the question. He'd then silently answer us by continuing to enjoy his ice cream until the empty plastic cup clattered to the floor.

Throughout his life with us, whenever he was examined by a veterinarian, they would always declare him to be "remarkable". Even as he got older.

Because of his short stature and his bad rear leg, whenever Beauregard wanted to get up on the couch or into the easy chair, he would plant his two front paws up onto the seat and wait until my wife or myself boosted him up.

Whenever I came home from work, Beauregard would immediately select one of his many toys, trot to the side door and wait for me to open it so we could go out and play. Among his favorite toys was a stuffed squirrel. One day I came home and there was one-too-many lifeless squirrels sprawled upon the floor – one of which was not stuffed.

When we were outside and he wanted to play, he would approach me with a grin and with his tail enthusiastically slapping back and forth. He would do a sudden head or body jerk – a fake, a juke, trying to spark me into playing with him.

Occasionally, Beauregard would get a gleam in his eye and would initiate mischief.

One of the more reoccurring instances was when I'd be working long hours on the computer in our home office and he had determined that I had been working long enough.

I would hear the approaching "click, click, click" of his paws against the hall tile floor as he determinedly strode from the living room. I would hear him take two steps into the office as he firmly planted his two front paws with an intended, distinctive clatter as he stopped, awaiting my response.

I'd wait a few seconds, and would turn around in my chair and there he'd be: tail a-wag with a mischievous gleam in his eye. If I did not immediately push away from the desk and get up, he would begin to bark until I did so.

Aside from lengthy sunbaths which he loved, Beauregard abhorred baths of any other kind. He was a typical boy. He hated baths and loved dirt. He loved lying in the shaded dirt craters which he had excavated in the backyard. Dirt was often his fragrance du jour.

Whenever my wife or I were blow-drying our hair after a shower, Beauregard would always show up for what we called his "hair dryer treatment". He would patiently wait until we directed the flow of the hair dryer on him so he could enjoy several minutes of the generated warmth.

I called him "Beau-Buddy" because he often seemed to genuinely want to help me with my work around the house. Speaking of which, he hated lawn mowers, weed whackers, vacuum cleaners or any tool or appliance which made a loud noise. The louder the machine's noise, the louder he'd bark.

Amazingly, as he got older, at seven every evening he would approach me and prompt me to escort him to bed by clawing my leg. His instinct for knowing when it was seven p.m. or very near it, was incredible. Once I walked him to his bed, I had to stay there until he fell asleep. If I left the room before he had fallen asleep, he would come get me and we would start the routine all over again.

As he aged, his muzzle whitened, but he kept his trim physique and weight, although his eyesight was failing him. He never lost his sweet disposition. Even when racked with cancer.

It broke our hearts when the time came time to say "goodbye" to him. We were extremely blessed to have had him as a family member for thirteen years. Thirteen years of the golden times. He truly enriched our lives.

He was our buddy. He was our sweet boy. More than that, he was remarkable.

FIFTY-THREE
BUTTER GIRL

We'd known the dog all of half an hour, had written a check, signed some papers and had promptly pulled her aboard, into the limited confines of the cabin of a Toyota Camry for the two-hour trip home. Now she was in the backseat, growling at our male Basset Hound in the front seat. I was envisioning hurtling north on I-75, attempting to maintain control of the automobile while a calamitous, alpha dog-establishing dog fight ensued.

The folks at the rescue organization had informed us that the large, primarily white, adult female Basset with the butterscotch-colored patches had been shuffled from foster home to foster home. She was approximately two years old. The previous owner had appropriately named her "Butterscotch".

We had initially seen Butterscotch in a photo on the rescue org's website. She was posed running happily in a field of green. My wife fell in love, and we arranged a no-obligation meeting with the rescue folks at a restaurant along I-75 in Florida. When they brought her out of their car, I was astounded at the dog's substantial height and overall size. After a few minutes of my wife holding the large dog on a leash, I attempted to discourage her, "She's awful big for a Basset Hound. You really don't want <u>her</u> do you?" It was then that my wife's face lit up with a big smile, "Oh yes, I do".

Somehow, we managed to get home without a dog fight. Thwarted perhaps because our male had tactfully retreated, cowering down onto the front floorboard, out of Butterscotch's line of sight.

Three or four times while at home that evening Butterscotch went after Beauregard, the male rescue Basset we'd had for a year. Fortunately, no blood was drawn, but Beauregard was terrified and hid in our bedroom, shaking. I told my wife that I would call the rescue organization in the morning and make arrangements to return Butterscotch.

At bedtime that evening, while my wife and Beauregard waited for me behind a closed bedroom door, I found Butterscotch stretched out on the living room couch. I crouched down next to her and spoke to her as if she were human, as her dark eyes studied me, "Sorry, but we can't have you attacking Beauregard, so we're going to have to return you in the morning. Sorry it didn't work out."

Just as I was about to rise and walk away, Butterscotch reached out her left paw toward me, as if to say "I'm not so bad. Give me another chance." I smiled and patted her paw, amazed and slightly moved, but steadfast in my decision, as I rose and returned to the bedroom.

"We've got to give her another chance," my wife stated after I related the paw incident to her. "No, she goes back in the morning," I replied firmly.

Our discussion continued the next morning during which I finally agreed to "a trial run". A trial run which would last nearly eleven years.

In her first few weeks with us she was standoff-ish, kept mostly to herself, drank out of the toilet, and restlessly roamed the halls and the rooms of the house at night, trying to adjust to her new home and to her new surroundings. In the beginning, she growled at her mom and growled and snapped if anyone got near her food when she was eating. To the end, she would steal "her brother" Beauregard's treats if he was not eating them fast enough. It took several months for her to warm up to us and to Beauregard.

Although her previous owners had formally named her "Butterscotch", as we became closer to her, we began to call her "Butter" and "Butter Girl".

Her short, white fur was extremely soft, as was often pointed out by the neighborhood kids whenever we took her for a walk. Sometimes they would point out the large patch of butterscotch-colored fur on her side which was in the shape of a heart. Her ears were long, brown, broad, and dangled. While her front paws were average size for a Basset Hound, her rear paws were small and dainty. She hated cats, loved baths, and often sashayed when she walked. Whenever she was curled up in a deep sleep, her soft, pink tongue protruded from her mouth a couple of inches.

Butter Girl was also a dancer. She would dance happily at the front door when she knew she was going for a walk. She would also wait outside her mom's bedroom door in the early morning, sometimes softly crying for her. Once her mom awakened and opened her bedroom door, Butter Girl would happily prance and dance in the hallway. No doubt in anticipation of her oncoming breakfast and of all the wonderful foods and treats which she would experience and enjoy during the new day. She was a happy girl.

Butter Girl was definitely a "foodie". The proverbial chow hound. Her favorite room in the house was the kitchen. She constantly kept the kitchen and its contents under surveillance. Grocery store days were among her favorite days. She would always insist on inspecting the incoming food and would personally escort every grocery item to its proper place in the house. At four o'clock every afternoon, Butter Girl could be found in the proximity of the kitchen, often lying beneath the dining room table, waiting for her evening meal which was typically served around five.

When not eating, Butter Girl spent a great deal of her personal time attempting to do so, by begging for food. She had it down to an effective science. She would intensely peer at either her mom or her dad for half an hour or more at a time, patiently, and determinedly shifting her weight from side to side so that we would be sure and catch her movement and know that she was there. She would amplify her efforts with sound: sometimes a pleading series of soft gentle cries; sometimes by implementing a soft, slurping sound, perhaps in anticipation of her soon-to-be acquired snack.

Butter Girl had an affinity for bathrooms. Inside the house, her favorite place to lay was on the cool tile floor of the main bathroom, between the toilet and the bathtub. In the middle of our taking showers in the master bath, she would often appear in the bathroom, lying down just outside the glass shower doors. There were a few occasions over the years where we found her inside the shower, lying on the shower floor.

Outside, her favorite place to lay was a concave dirt hole she had happily dug for herself in a flowerbed along a wall in the backyard. Whenever she would get excited outside, she would run into that hole and excitedly scurry her two front paws in the bottom of that hole, churning out an ample cloud of dirt and dust behind her. The more excited she was, the faster she worked, and the deeper the hole got.

In the beginning, she had understandably been a restless, distant, canine introvert, shuffled from foster home to foster home, who in time became a happy dog who loved and appreciated her selective bonding time with her human "parents". Bonding time with her dad often occurred in the morning when he was shaving, while she often bonded with her mom by jumping up onto the couch and climbing into her lap. All sixty pounds of her.

Although she was deaf during the last two or three years of her life, no matter where she was in the house, somehow whenever the refrigerator door opened, she was there.

She would then poke her head inside the door in order to capture all of the wonderful scents within.

To the end, Butter remained a happy girl, even though she had entered into old age and had acquired a multitude of warts, bumps, and lumps over her body. Whenever a new one appeared, we ran her into the vet and had it checked out. She received the best medical care money could buy.

We figured we saved her four times. The first when we rescued her from the pound. The second a few years later when a series of lumps appeared on the top of her head and a gifted veterinary surgeon saved her by removing the cancerous tumors. The third by having a precancerous outside toe removed on her right front foot, and the fourth occurring when her mom coaxed her back from the middle of a busy road, after she had gotten away.

We tried to save her a fifth time, but it didn't work. One day her right rear foot suddenly appeared to be bloody, as if she might have injured it in some way. We ran her into the vet the next day and we were told that it was cancer and that it was also in her lymph node behind her knee and that her spleen was enlarged. We had saved her so many times before. Surely, we could save her again.

We rushed Butter to an out-of-town veterinarian oncologist who gave her some IV chemo treatments. When that failed to impact the growth of the tumor, the oncologist recommended an oral at-home chemo treatment, but that also failed to impact the continued growth of the tumor.

Through what had to be the intense, throbbing pain of her foot, the effects of the chemo poison, occasionally shivering, and having to wear a cone around her neck 24/7 to prevent her from going after her afflicted foot, Butter Girl never cried, whined, or moped. She always kept coming. She always had heart, a drive, and an enthusiasm, which she had during her entire life with us. She had a great spirit. She soldiered through it all without complaint.

In the end, she had to have been in misery, roaming the halls and rooms of the house at night, much like she had when we had first gotten her, although now certainly in pain, constantly crashing and scraping her head-encased plastic cone into the many objects in her path.

After a complete assessment by our local vet who was in close communication with the oncologist, we were informed what we'd already known in our hearts. There was no hope. They recommended that we take Butter away from her pain and her misery.

When they brought us into the room to say goodbye to Butter Girl, she was still a happy girl. Full of energy and enthusiasm, wagging her tail, saying "hello" to everyone, despite her physical state. That made the gut-wrenching task even more difficult. To take away the life of such a sweet, passionate, positive, loving spirit. But then, there was the pain. We had to take her away from the pain and the misery.

By our request, the veterinarian who put Butter Girl down was the same doctor who had taken care of her for years and had saved her all those years ago by removing the cancerous tumors from her head. The doctor said she considered it an honor to be the one to take Butter Girl away from her pain.

In memoriam, a good friend of ours sent us a personalized wind-chime which we have hanging from a bush near Butter's final resting place. A small, simple, flat piece of wood dangles from the bottom of the chime which reads "When you hear the wind, think of me. In your heart I'll always be. Butter Girl".

Although there was no wind the day my wife and I gathered in our backyard for the burial of Butter Girl's ashes, just before we started, a light breeze suddenly arrived, gently tinkling the chrome, hollow tubes of the windchime. "That's Butter talking to us," my wife said with a broad, knowing smile.

We buried her ashes in the hole in which she loved to lay, appropriately along a border of delicate, pink flowers.

PART 13
IN MEMORIAM

FIFTY-FOUR
ELVIS, LEWIS, AND ERMA BOMBECK

I had a couple of chances to see Elvis perform back in the '70's. I didn't go. "I can always see Elvis," I said. "Elvis will be around forever."

I didn't read every timely new column that I could have by the late, syndicated humor columnist Lewis Grizzard when he was around. "I can always read Lewis," I said. "Lewis will be around forever."

Nor did I take the opportunity to read every fresh, new column by the late, syndicated humor columnist Erma Bombeck when she was alive, either. "I can always read Erma," I said. "Erma will be around forever."

As we get older, supposedly we get wiser.

Supposedly.

Three gifted people giving pleasure, happiness, and hope to so many of us.

Elvis pretty much self-destructed on the front nine, but it seems like Lewis and Erma should have had many more rounds of play.

For many years we were lucky. We had Lewis Grizzard and Erma Bombeck walking alongside of us, helping us get through everything from national calamities to missing socks. Often with a dash of humor.

Through their work and their humor, Grizzard and Bombeck brightened the world. Now, we must continue our journeys without them. There will be no more timely new columns or new books from them to help get us through.

Their passings were a double-whammy – both passing away within two years of one another.

They both died as they lived. With courage. Both facing not only life's everyday challenges, but also years of significant challenges of health.

Sometimes courage is what writing humor is all about. Reaching down inside yourself, even when times are tough, and pulling something out and writing a column about it. Even though it hurts.

Like this one.

Next chance I get, I'm gonna go see Elvis.

FIFTY-FIVE
RETURNING TO MAYBERRY

My Dad once said he never really cared for Andy Griffith. He told me he'd read somewhere that as an actor, Griffith was hard to work with. While my dad would have been the first to admit that he was no expert on Griffith's professional temperament, all I can say is that as an adult watching reruns of The Andy Griffith Show, there are occasional moments when Andy's character's mood appears to be much darker than it needs to be.

That said, I loved Andy Griffith and I loved watching the Andy Griffith Show. They were both an important part of my life.

Watching the Andy Griffith Show as a young boy growing up in the 60's, I always related to Opie, as we were about the same age, and I always looked upon Andy as a wise, even-handed, benevolent father figure. Over the years as I watched the show, Opie and I got older, and so did our dads.

In one of my favorite episodes, Opie, carelessly experimenting with a slingshot, kills a momma bird, leaving her three babies motherless. With Andy's guidance, Opie dutifully takes on the responsibility of raising the three baby birds. Toward the end of the show, the caged young birds are ready to fly. After a gentle, nudging conversation with Andy out on the porch, Opie realizes that he has to let them go. He hesitantly removes their cage from the porch, opens the cage door and one by one, delicately tosses each young bird into the air.

The little birds all successfully fly up into the trees around them.

"The cage sure looks awful empty, don't it, Pa?" Opie asks, to which Andy replies

"Yes son, it sure does. But don't the trees seem nice and full?"

In 1968, the Andy Griffith Show ended. Andy and Opie were gone. They left Mayberry and went off to Hollywood to find other work. The series that had helped define America and everything America stood for was over. Not even the TV spinoff Mayberry R.F.D. co-starring a smattering of the original Andy Griffith Show characters could ease the loss.

Back in the 80's I remember seeing a TV interview in which Andy was asked if he would ever consider doing a reunion show. A question he'd probably been asked hundreds of times.

He said he would not want to do a reunion show "just to do it". He went on to say that the story and the script would have to be right in order for them to agree to do the show.

Finally, in 1986 America's warm and wonderful town of Mayberry came back to life, and the surviving cast of beloved characters returned to television for one night, via the made for TV movie "Return to Mayberry". In the opening scene, a light-colored four-door sedan with Ohio license tags slowly and determinedly pursues the gentle twists and turns of an elevated, country road, gradually pulling over and parking alongside the road.

Andy emerges from the driver's seat, walks around to the passenger side of the empty car and leans against it, thoughtfully gazing down upon Myers Lake, as the familiar, iconic, whistled TV theme of the Andy Griffith Show sounds, and the screen nostalgically flashes back to the vintage black and white 1960's opening of the show where Andy and Opie are walking along the shore of the lake, fishing poles over their shoulders, as Opie stops and tries to skim a rock across the lake's surface.

Andy is home again, and so are we. As he thoughtfully studies the scene below, a broad, satisfying grin brightens his face. I can't help but wonder that if in addition to acting at that particular moment, Griffith isn't also fondly recalling the eight-year portion of his acting career which he spent as Mayberry's sheriff.

While 1986's Return to Mayberry was the last official production of The Andy Griffith Show, I have returned there many times. Mayberry was quaint and simple.

Uncomplicated, like its residents. The way we want real life to be, but it seldom is. Whenever my real life gets too complicated, I think back to the beautiful simplicity and to the innocence of Mayberry.

Late one evening, shortly after Andy Griffith's passing, I found myself outside and alone, gazing wistfully upward into the clear night sky, recalling the enjoyment which Griffith's performances had given me as a boy, all those years ago. As I reflected on his passing and the passing of so many other TV greats who'd entertained me throughout my child-hood, I studied the hundreds of bright stars shining downward from above. Yes, Griffith and those TV greats are gone, but don't the heavens seem nice and full?

FIFTY-SIX

DOUBLE T AND THE KING OF THE COWBOYS

Saturday mornings back in the early 1960's, I used to ride with Roy Rogers, King of the Cowboys. My young heart would soar with excitement at the opening of his tv show as Roy blazed across the screen at full gallop, mounted atop Trigger his faithful golden palomino, diligently popping off a few rounds from his immaculately polished six-shooter while in pursuit of some off-screen bad guys.

I loved the ride and the adventure, but in the mid-sixties the re-runs stopped. I grew older, turned in my semi-metallic six-guns and eventually rode off into adolescence, then adulthood, leaving behind all but the memories.

In 1977, I graduated college in the mountains of Western Maryland and moved a thousand miles south to my paternal grandparents' home in Florida. That year for my twenty-second birthday, my brother bought me my first Jimmy Buffett album. From my boyhood fandom of Roy Rogers, in my young adulthood I eagerly and figuratively stepped aboard the Euphoria, a 33-foot ketch sailboat owned by one James William Buffett who'd just released an album titled "Changes in Latitudes, Changes in Attitudes". That's "Buffett" with two t's.

A local realtor who'd guided my mom and dad in their purchase of their Florida house and who had befriended our family, not only introduced me to broader latitudes of Jimmy Buffett music, but also to the southern tradition of wearing shoes without socks.

After enthusiastically plunging into the tropical tunes and the laid-back lifestyle of Jimmy Buffett music, in 1977 I felt a calling to plant my bare feet in the fertile sands from which many of his songs had sprung. To make an artistic pilgrimage down to Key West, a.k.a. Cayo Hueso, a.k.a. Bone Island, a.k.a. the southernmost point in the U.S.

The drive from Key Largo to Key West was mesmerizing and unforgettable, as it still is today. Two hours of ocean on either side of the narrow ribbon of a highway, painted with breathtaking multitudes of gorgeous varying blues and greens. A spectacular kaleidoscope of God's pastels, the shades of which I could never have imagined. All illuminated by the beaming golden rays of an intense tropical sun.

Back then Key West was still somewhat rustic, unvarnished, and yet romantic. It still had a bit of an edge. It emanated an air of potential intrigue around each corner.

Perhaps a nod to its historic, somewhat shady past, more than a few apparently indigent characters still wandered the narrow streets and bars, searching for their next beer, providing a rich, deep well and aura from which Buffett could draw material for dozens of songs and stories.

In 1981, at the Lakeland Civic Center, Lakeland, Florida, I attended my first Jimmy Buffett concert. I still have the T-shirt, although these many years and a multitude of forkfuls later, the shirt is more than a few sizes past fitting me. If I recall correctly, the concert's special effects were basic, consisting of two imitation palm trees positioned on opposite sides at the back of the stage with a single wire stretched between them,celebrating The Coconut Telegraph tour.

Also in 1981, Buffett and Florida Governor Bob Graham founded the Save The Manatee Club of which I promptly became a member.

During one of my trips to Key West in the early eighties, I unexpectedly discovered an actual Jimmy Buffett store where you could buy Jimmy Buffett T-shirts when he wasn't on tour. What a concept! The store was long and very narrow, with a door on the back wall which featured a large A1A road sign which Governor Graham had presented to Buffett.

I remember speaking to store employee and Buffett friend Sunshine

Smith about how disappointed I was that all of the members of the band which had recorded on the "You Had To Be There" album had not remained to record the next. She explained that they were <u>a band</u> and that band members come and go. I understood, of course, but I was still disappointed.

When I returned a couple of years later and observed some construction in two adjacent stores on Duval Street, I went back to the T-shirt shop on the other part of the island and was told that Jimmy was going to open a restaurant in that construction space on Duval and was going to move the tee shirt shop there, as well. Soon Buffett fans would be able to enjoy a Cheeseburger in Paradise at the restaurant, then be able to walk next door and buy a tee shirt. What a concept!

Over the years visiting Key West I figured that one day I might run into Jimmy Buffett, but it never happened. From my experience, trying to run into Jimmy Buffett in Key West in the eighties and beyond was a lot like the line you hear when you get skunked fishing – "You should have been here yesterday". Although a few times I did run into Captain Tony at his saloon, once he initiated a conversation about the ERA with my cousin and me.

Although I have attended many Jimmy Buffett concerts over the years, if someone were to ask me "how many?" I would have to respond, "not enough". He left us a lot of great times and great tunes. Hardly a day goes by that I don't sing at least one Jimmy Buffett song to myself. For decades, his music has enriched my life and so, has been a significant part of my life and to those of my friends.

Somewhere along the line, the Buffett fan population surged, and became dubbed "Parrotheads" with tens of millions of members listed on the ship's manifest.

Buffett's musical legacy is a gift, much of it initially borne from the sands and soil of Key West, Florida. No matter where you live or if you've never been, if you listen close enough, some of the songs on his early albums can take you back to that simpler, laidback lifestyle of the Key West of long ago. Back to a place where life moved just a little bit slower. Back to a place where people were livin' and dyin' in three-quarter time.

Reflecting on the life of Jimmy Buffett, I cannot help but think of the photo on the back of his 1979 Volcano album. He is seated on the rocky terrain of a smoldering volcano, pointing to the smoke bellowing outward next to him as he sports a big grin. The photo's caption is the mantra by which he lived his life.

The caption reads: "Ain't Life Grand".

Ain't it though?

PART 14
EPILOGUE

I WISH SATURDAY NIGHTS COULD
LAST FOREVER

In the movie "Hooper", starring Burt Reynolds as an aging veteran Hollywood stuntman, and Jan-Michael Vincent as his young, up-and-coming protege, there is a climactic movie stunt scene in which they are both strapped into the front bucket seats of a single, specially outfitted "rocket car", about to attempt to "fly" the car 325 feet in the air, in a truly death-defying feat over a huge, gaping gorge.

At first, inside the car everything's going great, until just before take-off, cameras rolling, they see that their car's rocket engine is rapidly beginning to lose pressure.

Cameras still rolling, Jan-Michael Vincent stops the car when he notes the precarious loss of pressure. Then, he realizes that despite the odds, he and Burt are going anyway. It's what they're supposed to do.

A minute later, they ignite the rocket engine and are slammed forward, up into the air, and successfully sail over the gorge.

Sometimes real life is a lot like that Burt Reynolds movie. Like it or not, sometimes we go anyway.

That is what we're here to do today.

It's hard for me to believe that I've been writing for "Heartbeat Magazine" for nine years. It all began with a horse. A vile, cantankerous, biting-oriented, Puerto Rican horse named "Coco", which - it is my sincere and fervent hope at this late date, is generously contributing to the fertilization of a prosperous Puerto Rican sugarcane field, from a prone, subterranean position.

I suppose the origin and the experience for writing that horse story truly began in Prattville, Alabama in 1963, when Mrs. White marched an extremely shy, little tow-headed boy who had been writing in class when he should have been listening, to the front of the room as punishment, in order to read aloud what he'd been writing, the contents of which miraculously caused the more intellectually affluent members of that third-grade class to chuckle and laugh.

I've been writing ever since. The difference is for the last nine years, I've been privileged enough to have had you to "read" too. Over those years, on at least one occasion, I hope to have made you laugh. Maybe even made you think.

Maybe brought a lump to your throat.

Mainly, I hope to have made you laugh. If only once.

I have met some great people through my efforts at "Heartbeat Magazine", including Kathy Nicklaus Adkins, the magazine's creator, founder, original Publisher and Editor. The wonderful, generous lady who "took a chance on a horse" and gave me my start with the publication.

My sincere thanks also to the magazine's final Publisher and Editor, Mona Jackson and her sister, Assistant Editor Dina Jackson, two gifted, hardworking ladies who are not only wonderful people, but also very dear friends.

I would also like to express my sincere thanks to nationally syndicated columnist, bestselling author, and Pulitzer Prize winner Dave Barry for his kindness and for his support over the years. His humor makes the world a brighter place.

While I have been published in other magazines and in newspapers, "Heartbeat" has always been "home" to me. Like the movie says, "There's no place like home".

Now, "home" is going away.

It has been both an honor and a privilege to have attempted to "tickle your ivories".

I wish Saturday nights could last forever.

But they can't.

I wish "Heartbeat Magazine" could last forever.

But it couldn't.

In the spirit that I might one day be able to return in order to publicly lob forth a few more tomaters your way, I would call upon the habitual episode-closing words – with a twist - of the eternally cool Jack Lord, a.k.a. Steve McGarrett, 1970's TV icon, and star of the original Hawaii Five-O, by invoking a Hawaiian word which appropriately not only serves as a greeting, but also as a fond "farewell":

Be there.

Aloha.

ABOUT THE AUTHOR

Drew Snell is retired and is currently living in Southwest Florida. He has also lived in Southeast Florida, Central Florida, France, Michigan, Massachusetts, Alabama, Nebraska, Puerto Rico, and Maryland. He is tired of moving and is happy to say that he no longer has United Van Lines on speed dial.

He has had many articles and stories published and is the author of Belly-Up, a mystery/adventure novel which is currently available on Amazon. He is currently at work on another novel.

www.ingramcontent.com/pod-product-compliance
Lightning Source LLC
Chambersburg PA
CBHW060012050426

42448CB00012B/2717